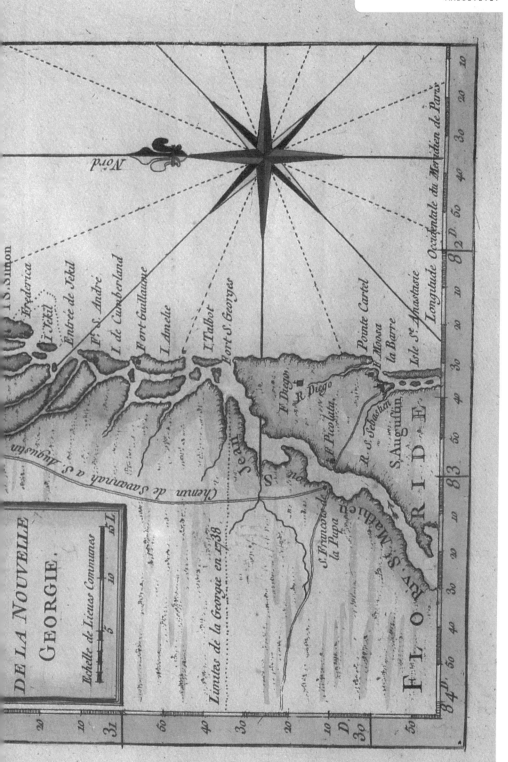

DE LA NOUVELLE GEORGIE.

Echelle de Lieuas Communes

Nord

I. S. Simon
Frederica
I. Jekil
Entrée de Jekil
F. S. André.
I. de Cumberland
Fort Guillaume
I. Amelie
I. Talbot
Fort S. Georges

Pointe Cartel
H. Moosa
la Barre
Isle S. Anastasie
Longitude Occidentale du Meridien de Paris

F. Diego
R. Diego
H. Picolata
R. S. Sebastian
S. Augustin

S. Francois
la Pupa

R. S. Jean

Chemin de Savannah a S. Augustin

Limites de la Georgie en 1738

FLORIDE.

R. S. Mathieu

Journal of a Visit to the Georgia Islands of St. Catherines, Green, Ossabaw, Sapelo, St. Simons, Jekyll, and Cumberland,

with Comments on the Florida Islands
of Amelia, Talbot, and St. George,
in 1753

Jonathan Bryan (1708–1788)

*J*ournal of a Visit to the Georgia Islands of St. Catherines, Green, Ossabaw, Sapelo, St. Simons, Jekyll, and Cumberland,

with Comments on the Florida Islands of Amelia, Talbot, and St. George, in 1753

Virginia Steele Wood
and
Mary R. Bullard, editors

MERCER UNIVERSITY PRESS
In association with
The Georgia Historical Society
1996

ISBN 0-86554-490-5

Journal of a Visit to the Georgia Islands
edited by Virginia Steele Wood and Mary R. Bullard

"Journal of a Visit to the Georgia Islands" original manuscript
is the property of the Georgia Historical Society.
This edition copyright © 1996 Mercer University Press.
All rights reserved.

Library of Congress Cataloging-in-Publication Data

Bryan, Jonathan, 1708–1788.
    Journal of a visit to the Georgia Islands of St. Catherines, Green, Ossabaw, Sapelo,
St. Simons, Jekyll, and Cumberland, with comments on the Florida islands of Amelia,
Talbot, and St. George, in 1753 / Virginia Steele Wood and Mary R. Bullard, editors.
    xvii + 103   7x10"
    Includes bibliographical references and index.
    ISBN 0-86554-490-5   (alk. paper)
    1. Golden Isles (Ga.)—Description and travel—Early works to 1800. 2. Golden Isles
(Ga.)—Social life and customs.   3. Sea Islands—Description and travel—Early works
to 1800. 4. Islands—Georgia—History—18th century. 5. Islands—Florida—History—
18th century. 6. Bryan, Jonathan, 1708–1788—Diaries.   I. Wood, Virginia S.
II. Bullard, Mary Ricketson.   III. Title.
F292.G58B79   1996
975.8'742—dc20   96-5743
                                                                          CIP

Contents

Foreword *by Louis De Vorsey, Jr.* ix

Preface *by Virginia Steele Wood and Mary R. Bullard* xi

Introduction *by Virginia Steele Wood and Mary R. Bullard* 1

The Journal 17

Short Titles, Abbreviations, and Location Symbols 35

Notes 57

Credits 93

Index 95

Notes on the Contributors 103

To the Memory
of
LILLA MILLS HAWES
Director Emerita
of the
Georgia Historical Society

JOURNAL OF A VISIT TO THE GEORGIA ISLANDS is published in association with the Georgia Historical Society. Founded in 1839, The Society's mission is to collect, preserve, and share Georgia history and to maintain an historical research library for its members and the public. Designated a branch depository of the Georgia Department of Archives and History in 1966, the Society publishes the *Georgia Historical Quarterly* in conjunction with the University of Georgia and holds a number of workshops and historical lectures throughout the state. For additional information, please write the Georgia Historical Society, 501 Whitaker Street, Savannah, Georgia 31499, or call the Society at (912) 651-2125.

Foreword

he heart of this book is the journal kept by a mid-eighteenth-century explorer of coastal Georgia. He was, what we might term today, a "mover and shaker." Jonathan Bryan was an entrepreneur rather than a natural scientist or gentleman traveler, the more familiar chroniclers of that age. He was in the vanguard of the migration of economically successful, but politically frustrated, South Carolina planters to neighboring Georgia. Bryan's decision to invest his fortunes there had a major impact on that colony's recovery from its near collapse in the waning years of the Georgia Trust's well-intentioned but failed administration.

William Gerard De Brahm, a German-born cartographer–military engineer accompanying Bryan on his exploratory tour, was painfully near the truth when he wrote, in 1751, that had it not been "for the few English in the Government['s] Employ, and the Salzburgers, [I] . . . would have found this Province intirely deserted in Inhabitants. . . . " In addition to insuring the economic viability of the newly organized royal colony, Bryan and his fellows were responsible for a dramatic racial shift that still marks Georgia's demographic profile. As De Brahm noted, "the spirit of Emigration out of South Carolina into Georgia became so universal [in 1752] that [in] this and the following year near one thousand Negroes were brought in Georgia, where in 1751 were scarce above three dozen." While Bryan did not identify them in his journal, a number of Negro slaves were very likely in the large party he led along the coastal waterway protected by Georgia's range of barrier islands; most probably they were the "Sixteen hands" accompanying planter William Simmons to his heavily wooded land grant near the head of today's aptly named Serpent River.

By 1752–1753 De Brahm was acquiring land for himself, and his mapping skills were already well-known and respected. Exactly how he came to be accompanying Bryan on this journey to the "southward" is not revealed in the documents. Interestingly, however, this trip—De Brahm's third along the coast but previously undocumented—sheds light on what had earlier been something of a cartographic mystery. Both his highly regarded printed maps of 1757 and 1780 show "St. Andrews Fort" near rather than actually on Cumberland Island. As Bryan's journal reveals, De Brahm became ill after he reached Fort St. Andrews on Cumberland Island. He was taken to Frederica before the party reached the Dividings River and therefore had no opportunity to view this waterway at firsthand. Had De Brahm traveled southward in the next few days with the others, he would have noticed that the fort site stood north of the desemboguement of Dividings River and on Cumberland itself. Without Bryan's journal the reason for De Brahm's misplacement of Fort St. Andrews would remain a minor historical mystery.

Like all explorers, Jonathan Bryan and his fellows were assessing the area he described from a particular point of view. Thanks to the meticulous scholarly research of editors Mary R. Bullard and Virginia Steele Wood, readers of this journal are carried into Bryan's world and time and made aware of that point of view. It was a time and world marked by great and accelerating change—a time and world not unlike our own. Bryan's journal provides a colorful and informative glimpse of colonial Georgia's coastal zone at the moment of its economic takeoff as a lucrative rice-producing region. Bryan, William Simmons, and scores of their fellow South Carolinians were the founders of an economic and social system that would characterize the region for the next century. Echoes of that system still resonate through the marshes and barrier islands of present-day Georgia.

Louis De Vorsey, Jr.

Preface

n the first sentence of his unsigned journal, the author of the document that follows identified himself when he wrote these words on 6 August 1753: "We left my Plantation at Indian Land[1] in South Carolina and arrived at my Plantation at Walnut Hill in Georgia the next day." As the sole owner of Walnut Hill plantation since 1751, and the owner of three large plantations on South Carolina's old Indian Lands, Jonathan Bryan (1708–1788)[2] is the only person who could have made that statement. By 1753 his acumen and driving energy had propelled him from relative obscurity to the threshold of wealth and influence. He was a remarkable individual. In a life that spanned eighty years, he was an outstanding participant in America's southern frontier development—from colony to independence—and his involvement in the myriad aspects of Georgia's early history is well documented in Alan Gallay's biography, *The Formation of the Planter Elite: Jonathan Bryan and the Southern Frontier.*[3]

Facts concerning the provenance of Bryan's hitherto unpublished journal are meager. In 1847, when Dr. William Bacon Stevens (1815–1887) published the first volume of his *History of Georgia*, he described the 1755 tour of Gov. John Reynolds through southern Georgia. For St. Simons Island and Frederica he set the scene by quoting verbatim the poignant description of a visitor in 1753 who beheld "the melancholy prospect of houses without inhabitants, barracks without soldiers, guns without carriages, and streets grown over with weeds. All appeared to me with a very horrible aspect, and so different from what I once knew it, that I could scarce refrain from tears."[4]

Although Stevens attributed this passage to "an anonymous journalist," it is from Bryan's journal, and over the years it has been quoted by various historians.[5] Whether Stevens owned or borrowed the original manuscript from which this came (or a copy of it) is unknown, but he quite clearly had access to it during the 1840s, or earlier.

In his *History* Stevens also discussed the Bosomworth Controversy in which a merchant named Isaac Levy[6] was heavily involved. Stevens acknowledged that his account was "drawn entirely from manuscript and official sources . . . and a large package of valuable original papers, kindly furnished me by J. [I.] K. Tefft, Esq. of Savannah."[7] To date we have only one tentative link to those manuscripts. Some time after his selection as the historian of Georgia in 1824, Joseph Valence Bevan (1798–1830) planned to write an integrated history of the state. In this connection he acquired the "Thomas Bosomworth Controversy Manuscripts" from Georgia manuscript collector Israel Keech Tefft (1794–1862). Following Bevan's untimely death in 1830 his collected documents were sold, and the Bosomworth papers were acquired by the Library of Congress for the Peter Force Collection.[8]

In 1839 both Israel Tefft and William Stevens were deeply involved in helping establish the Georgia Historical Society. (The latter became its first recording secretary and later the librarian.) In 1867, five years after Tefft's death, most of his manuscript collection went to the auction block; the catalogue mentions no Bryan journal, although it may once have been in Tefft's possession.[9] Mr. and Mrs. Marmaduke Floyd of Savannah[10] probably acquired it during the 1940s, and their son, Picot Floyd, subsequently donated it in 1974 to the Georgia Historical Society, where it is part of the M. H. and D. B. Floyd Collection.

It is interesting and curious to note that the journal's inside cover bears this inscription in another hand: "Journal to and a Description of Georgia, especially of the Islands of St. Catherine, Osseba & Sappalo, of Which three islands I Levy owned a moiety." Following its acquisition by the Society in 1974, and based on that inscription, the journal was attributed to Isaac Levy and, understandably, cataloged under his name. The "I" in the inscription, however, is the initial letter of Levy's first name and not a pronoun. The editors found no evidence that Isaac Levy was ever a resident of South Carolina or Georgia, or that he procured any land in either colony or was an outdoorsman. He was, instead, the urban-dwelling son of an exceptionally wealthy New York merchant family and, to judge from his writing, was obviously well educated. It is difficult to conjure up an image of Levy embarking on a hazardous trip to cope for days at a time in the hostile, primitive environment that the group endured and that was related in this journal of 1753.

Jonathan Bryan, on the other hand, was a lifelong resident of the two southern-most colonies. Energetic and physically strong, he was adventurous and astute and was at various times a scout, surveyor, negotiator, soldier, planter, entrepreneur, politician, religious advocate, and patriot. He was knowledgeable about the myriad aspects of agriculture, sagacious in matters of law and diplomacy, acquisitive when it came to land, and adaptable in social settings. The journal's entries mesh with Bryan's experience and influence: being familiar with the coastal waterways, islands, and fortifications; gaining permission, apparently with ease, to use the colony's armed boat and crew; having no apparent difficulty living among and directing a rough and independent-minded group of armed men; experiencing no discernible anguish in the face of primitive outdoor living in the torrid, oppressive weather conditions; supporting the concept of settling emigré Dissenters on Georgia soil; renewing established friendships and acquaintances among the coastal residents; and, not least,

Company. of Rangers, and other Extra Company.,
has been the sole cause of this Place's declining
and sinking into Contempt and almost nothing;
the poor Inhabitants, whose Industry were encouraged. Family. supported and Property. defended
by the Regiment, are quite dispirited, and
mostly, removed quite away, and left their
Habitations, being afraid to expose themselves
and Family. to the Insults of their troublesom
Neighbours the Spainards —

   O Frederica! had thy Founder known,
The Calamitous Days that were to come,
Or had thy Genius let thy Builder see,
The secret purpose of Divine Decree,
How soon thy Walls defenceless should remain,
And those lofty Towers lavel'd to the Plain,
Thy Bastions once, whose Cannon thundred air,
To Neighbouring Spain, and Forida a Law,
To be disdain'd, not worthy Britain's Care
Had caus'd a Sigh, and forc'd a buing Tear.

Capt Demere has a Company (about Fifty
Men for this Place, but they were either
out on Detachments or upon Furloughs,
so that there was not as I was informed

A page from the journal

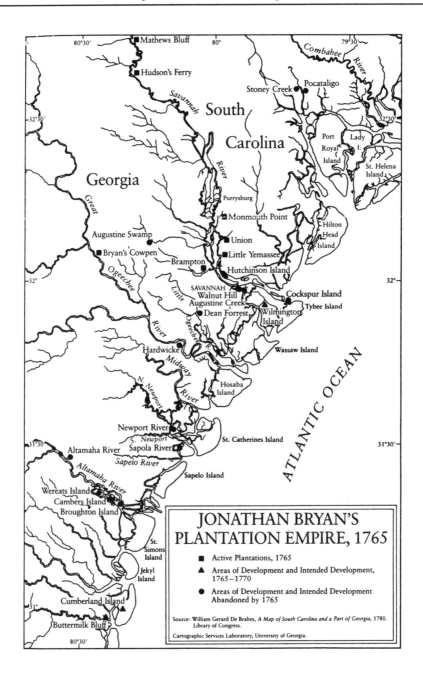

JONATHAN BRYAN'S
PLANTATION EMPIRE, 1765

■ Active Plantations, 1765

▲ Areas of Development and Intended Development,
1765–1770

● Areas of Development and Intended Development
Abandoned by 1765

Source: William Gerard De Brahm, *A Map of South Carolina and a Part of Georgia,* 1780.
Library of Congress.

Cartographic Services Laboratory, University of Georgia.

having the ability to evaluate the best land for raising livestock and for planting rice, corn, and indigo.

The brevity and exactness of the journal suggest that it was prepared as a report, perhaps for the benefit of Capt. John Reynolds, who assumed his new duties as royal governor in 1754. There was a precedent for such a document. For example, in 1721, following an expedition to construct Fort King George during which time he kept a daily record, Col. John Barnwell wrote to South Carolina's royal governor, Francis Nicholson, declaring that "the most Regular way of giving you an Account is to do So By way of [a] Journall."[11] From this vantage point one can rather easily construe the journal as a type of field report, but thus far the name of no individual or group has surfaced as the recipient of the author's effort.

Given the excellent condition of the manuscript—the careful handwriting, the absence of strikeouts, ink smudges, or water damage—it appears to be a fair copy rather than the original document written under adverse conditions during the journey. From rough notes it was, and still is, a "common practice" for authors to write their travel narratives or diaries on returning home and, with amendments, to make multiple copies to circulate among family and friends.[12] Certainly, Jonathan Bryan could well afford to engage a scribe or amanuensis to undertake the task of copying.

Written on laid paper, each leaf of the journal bears a similar watermark—*Pro Patria*, the Maid of Holland. It is a crude imitation of a motif commonly used by Dutch papermakers, but in this instance the specific papermaker has not been identified.[13]

Measuring 17.25 centimeters by 20 centimeters, the journal consists of twenty-five legible pages with one or more leaves missing between the entries dated 16 and 18 August 1753. It was transcribed exactly as written with all words supplied by the editors in square brackets. Emendations are relatively few, but we substituted periods for colons, added some commas, broke some long passages into paragraphs, and changed to the lower case all capital letters that appear in the middle of words. The notes amplify Jonathan Bryan's comments, thereby providing what the editors trust will be a heightened appreciation of his journal. We have chosen to use the double-dating method for dates falling between 1 January and 25 March before 1752. On 25 March in that year, Great Britain and the colonies changed from the Julian to the Gregorian calendar. Before then, New Year's Day fell on 25 March; hence our use of the solidus (slash) to indicate the old and the new date style.

We acknowledge with gratitude the keen interest and help of many people. Primarily, we are indebted to Anne P. Smith, library director of the Georgia

Historical Society, for encouraging us to edit the manuscript and giving us her enthusiastic support as the project progressed. The Society's archivists, Jan Flores and Eileen A. Ielmini, cheerfully and promptly answered our questions about material in manuscript collections, provided certain citations, and helped proofread our transcript against the original document.

We are indebted to Dr. Louis De Vorsey, Jr., professor emeritus, University of Georgia, for reading with care our entire manuscript, for raising some pertinent points for clarification, and for his generosity in writing the foreword.

Early in our work on the Bryan journal Dr. Edward J. Cashin of Augusta College, Dr. Alan Gallay of the University of Washington, and Dr. John T. Juricek of Emory University heightened our awareness of particular aspects of Georgia's colonial history.

W. M. P. Dunne, Long Island University; John J. MacDonough, Jr., Manuscript Division, Library of Congress; and Robert Seager II, former editor of the Henry Clay papers, read portions of the manuscript, and we gained much from their constructive criticism.

Those who gave us the benefit of pertinent comments about particular aspects of the journal include Dr. Frederick C. Marland, former chief, Coastal Protection, Georgia Department of Natural Resources, on dividings; Dr. Lawrence E. Babits, Program in Maritime History and Nautical Archaeology, Department of History, East Carolina University, on piraguas; Dr. Robert Rathburn, director, Jekyll Island Authority, on the William Horton house; Dr. W. A. B. Douglas, former director of general history, Canadian National Defence Headquarters, on the military career of Col. William Cooke; Dr. David M. Ludlum, Princeton, on the 1752 hurricanes; Marion R. Hemperley, formerly of Georgia's Surveyor-General Department, on geographical features; Patricia C. Barefoot, park ranger, Fort Frederica National Monument, National Park Service, on material from their files; and Fred C. Cook, on the present-day site of White Post. Others who are authorities in their chosen fields advised us: Muriel H. Parry on small sailing craft, particularly xebecs; Thomas L. Gravell on watermarks and paper of the colonial era; and Donald G. Ethrington, conservator, for his assessment of the age of this journal. Lara Lee Winchester, formerly at Fort Morris Historic Site (adjacent to old Sunbury, Georgia) and a specialist in colonial textiles, provided firsthand information about producing dye from indigo.

In addition, those who shared information from their files or helped in other ways include Francis Howell Beckemeyer, Robert S. Davis, Jr., Captain Alvin Dickey, Sr., Eugenia W. Howard Edwards, Newell T. Parr, Sarah N. Pinckney, John M. Sheftall, Kenneth H. Thomas, Jr., Mary Bondurant Warren, and Lisa L. White.

We commend staff members at the following institutions for their indispensable reference assistance: the Georgia Department of Archives and History; the Hargrett Rare Book and Manuscript Library, University of Georgia; the South Carolina Department of Archives and History; and the Jewish Archives. For their inestimable help on many occasions Virginia S. Wood especially thanks her colleagues at the Library of Congress in the Humanities and Social Sciences Division, Geography and Map Division, Manuscript Division, Rare Book Division, Law Library, and the Serials Division.

Virginia Steele Wood
Mary R. Bullard

Introduction

lthough Jonathan Bryan already owned large plantations northwest of Port Royal, on 20 September 1750 he petitioned the governing body of Georgia for "Five Hundred Acres of Marsh and Swamp land," across from Hutchinson Island, bounded "on the North by the Savannah River." Located five miles below Savannah itself, the tract was granted with alacrity by the President and Assistants in Council.[14] Bryan's decision to expand his holdings into Georgia was propitious. After the Trustees finally bowed to pressure in 1749 and permitted slavery in the colony, they abandoned entailment the following year in favor of fee simple conveyances, and in June 1752 they formally relinquished their colonial experiment to the crown.[15]

Georgia was eager to attract settlers, and for most adult white males land was available virtually for the asking although acreage was limited. The fertile swampland adjacent to certain tidal rivers was the most desirable to acquire, and the colony's governing body generally granted it to men with political influence who had the slaves, financial resources, vigor, and technical skill to undertake the complexities of rice production. Bryan qualified on all counts.[16]

At the beginning of January 1751 he began creating his new plantation out of the swamps south of Savannah, and two days after Christmas 1752 his family moved to a new home there which they called Walnut Hill.[17] Seven months later, shortly before his forty-fifth birthday, Bryan was poised and ready to revisit the southern coastal region, and in early August 1753 he set out with a small party on a "voyage of Discovery and Observation" as far south as they "thought proper to proceed." His journal is our only known legacy of that trip. It is a noteworthy addendum to his biography.

It was not, however, Bryan's initial foray beyond the boundaries of Savannah, for one can document at least four trips he made to the Georgia-Florida frontier prior to 1753. As a youth of twenty-one in 1728–1729, probably just after the attack against Yamasees in St. Augustine during the brief Anglo-Spanish War (1727–1728), he served on an expedition to the St. Johns River in Florida to reconnoitre that region. In 1733, concurrent with the arrival of James Oglethorpe and the first group of Georgia settlers, Bryan commanded the scout boat from Port Royal that patrolled the Inland Passage.[18] On St. Simons, he offered assistance to the colony as Frederica was being constructed under Oglethorpe's supervision.[19] Then in March 1736, again at Frederica, he reported that along "with Tomochichi Mico and several other persons he went to the . . . River of St. Wans [St. Johns]" where they saw no Spanish settlements.[20] Four years later, in the spring of 1740, Bryan led a small group of Carolina volunteers and Indians to support Oglethorpe's effort to conquer Spanish-held St. Augustine—an expedition that ended in grievous failure.[21] But the nature of Bryan's 1753 trip differed from a military operation.

His motivation for making the journey is not spelled out in the journal, but one may glean some clue of it from a letter he wrote on 1 July 1753, only a month before departure. He noted that "Georgia thrives apace and it will be Settled by the neighboring Colonies." He extolled her "Open ports Exempted from Duties which is a great Incouragement to trade" and praised the absence of taxes and quit rents. At the same time, however, he warned that "what I feer is when we come to have a Govr. and Assembly we Shall be too fond of Making Laws and perhaps, burthen our Selves with some unnecisary."[22] It is significant that Bryan initiated his trip some thirteen months before John Reynolds, the new royal governor, arrived from England, and it is impressive that during the decade following this trip he amassed so much land between the Savannah and Altamaha Rivers that he "could easily have walked from Savannah to Darien and spent every night of his journey on one of his own settlements."[23]

As Bryan and his boat crew set out that August day in 1753, the party included William Gerard De Brahm, cartographer, military engineer, and surveyor; and Bryan's brother-in-law John Williamson and William Simmons, both South Carolina planters. The Georgia that attracted this little band was a colony barely twenty years old and still struggling to survive. What they observed was little more than a quiet wilderness with some 4,043 individuals who comprised the population within a territory of about 1,800 square miles.[24] Indian treaties confined the settlers to an area 150 miles long by 30 miles wide along the coast (including the barrier islands) and a narrow, 125-mile strip as far as Augusta along the west bank of the Savannah River, the same waterway that marked the Georgia–South Carolina boundary. Most of these settlers worked small isolated farms and supplemented subsistence from their crops with livestock and wild game. Any who infringed beyond limits of the treaty trespassed on Indian hunting grounds, and retaliation was swift. To the south and west, beyond their immediate Indian neighbors, Spain and France claimed the territory.[25]

Savannah was the colony's largest town, but it boasted only a few hundred souls whose principal orientation was the river, since pine woods abutted the other three

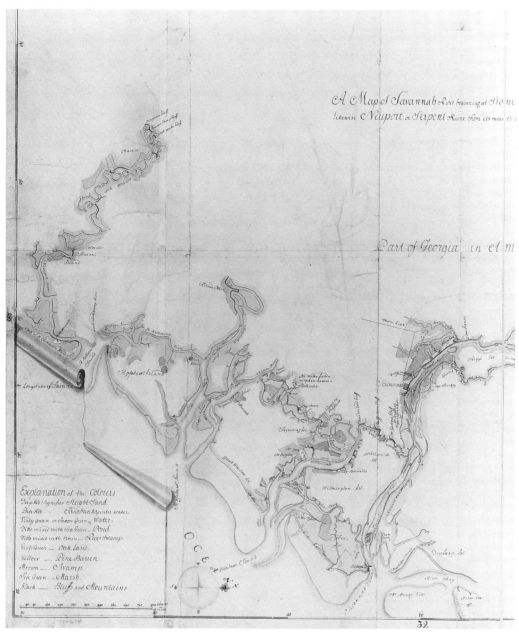

*The Island Passage from Savannah
to St. Catherines Island, Georgia (1752)*

sides. Because no surface rocks or stones are found in this coastal plain for some eighty miles inland, the colonists used the abundant timber for their dwellings and public buildings. For more durable construction they relied on tabby.[26] About ten miles up the river at Ebenezer was a settlement of Lutherans from Salzburg, mostly "a cluster of farm lots hemmed into the mud bottoms of the Savannah River and Ebenezer Creek by the ubiquitous pine barrens."[27] At Augusta, another ninety miles upriver, there were close to eighty houses, a church, and the dilapidated Fort Augusta that served as headquarters for the local troops as well as an Indian trading post.[28]

In a manner of speaking Georgia was in a state of limbo. The Trustees who established the colony in 1733 surrendered their charter on 24 June 1752, a year earlier than had been anticipated. A heated debate over reuniting Georgia with South Carolina came to nothing. On 24 November Georgia was proclaimed a royal province, although a two-year delay ensued until the crown's first governor arrived in October 1754. Commissioners of the Board of Trade and Plantations in London had charge during the interim, but they directed that all those serving in civil, military, and ecclesiastical capacities were to continue until the governor assumed his duties. For the colonists, it was a time of much apprehension about their future.[29]

It was along the periphery of the fertile southern frontier that Bryan and his companions began their passage below Savannah, visiting first at St. Catherines Island, partially occupied by the Bosomworths and probably several Indian families. They next visited the site of William Simmons's newly planned settlement up the Newport River where they spent several days surveying. Continuing on, some seventy miles south of Savannah, they explored the uninhabited island of Sapelo, but they bypassed Darien, the tiny river village settled by Highland Scots on a bluff overlooking the mighty Altamaha.

Their next stop along the coast was St. Simons Island. This was home to a few families, most of whom struggled to subsist following disbandment of the regiment at Fort Frederica in the spring of 1749. Although a small detachment of soldiers remained, Bryan found it painful to see the town in such "a ruinous condition." It presented to him a "melancholy Prospect of Houses without Inhabitants, Barracks without Soldiers, Guns without Carriages and the Streets grown over with Weeds." Moved by its "very horrible Aspect" he wrote a poem, a lament, for the Frederica he recalled in better days.

Since hostilities still simmered among the Spanish and their Indian allies in Florida, it was prudent to take precautions before continuing south. By order of the colony's president a scout boat with two swivel guns and "ten clever hearty Fellows double armed" joined the party for protection. The group proceeded to Jekyll Island

and inspected the Horton plantation. Although laid waste by retreating Spanish soldiers in 1742, it once again appeared to be flourishing. Farther along on Cumberland Island, adjacent to Spanish-held Florida, they found Fort St. Andrews at the north end abandoned and in ruins. Fort William with its lonely detachment— six soldiers and their corporal—stood at the south end. Damaged by the 1752 hurricane, it too, suffered neglect and, as Bryan noted, was "in a ruinous Condition."

Their only casualty was William De Brahm, who became ill and was taken back to Frederica in Bryan's boat. For the others, who transferred to the scout boat, Talbot and Fort St. George Islands at the mouth of the St. Johns River marked the southernmost limit of their exploration, which was curtailed by inclement weather. Back in Frederica they found De Brahm's health greatly improved. Then, under way once more and heading north on their return, the men were entertained by Adam Bosomworth on St. Catherines; they also visited Mark Carr's planned site of Sunbury; and at Green Island they called on the Maxwell family. Just before the end of August Jonathan Bryan arrived home, having been absent for nearly a month.

The conditions under which he and his contingent made their way along the coast were primitive and most of the time involved camping out, living off the country by fishing, and hunting deer and other game. As travelers in August they faced the sweltering heat and oppressive humidity of a semitropical climate that many find enervating and often debilitating. In the boats they endured battering by storms with dangerously high winds and torrential rains. Furthermore, they had virtually no defense against the assault of an "Abundance of . . . Torments," swarms of noxious insects, particularly mosquitoes, that emerge in force at dusk and plague their victims through the night and "whose Venom . . . according to their Bulk, is as baleful as that of a Rattle Snake."[30]

As a native son, enured to the exigencies of sultry southern summers and the insect population, Bryan never once complained or alluded to any personal discomfort. On the other hand he readily expressed compassion for members of his crew who were exposed to the elements on the upper deck, who "Suffer'd very much, being obliged to endure all the Hardship of Wind and Weather, and not the least Shelter." Before disbandment of the regiment at Frederica in 1749, they had been members of the Georgia Marine Company and were praised by Oglethorpe as "a hardy kind of Men thoroughly acquainted with all the Water Passages and row by Night and Day. They can live by fishing and shooting and are not easily to be prevailed with to Serve unless by Hope of large Gain. . . . They are as contented in Woods as in Houses. They are excellent scouts."[31] De Brahm, on the other hand, reached adulthood in the cooler climes of northern Europe. His indisposition on this

Drawing of a petiaqua
from the notebooks of Philip von Reck, 1730s

trip can perhaps be attributed, at least in part, to the heat, to their diet, and possibly to the "agues" endemic to the southern coastal region.[32]

The boat in which Bryan initiated his trip was barely mentioned, but his ten-man crew suggests strongly that it was a piragua, which would require a large crew to man the oars. Such vessels were in common use during the eighteenth century along the South Carolina–Georgia coast.[33] They were actually large dugout hulls, often carved from single cypress or cedar logs that were split in half lengthwise and fitted with a wide plank in the center. Some were thirty to over forty feet in length and five or more feet in width; the freeboard was increased with planks along the rail to increase capacity and to protect against spray and waves. They could easily transport a cargo of thirty-five tons or more. Although usually propelled by oars, the boats were also fitted with two masts rigged with Bermuda-type sails; they had no deck, but typically there was "a kind of forecastle and a cabin."[34] Given their shallow draft, piraguas were ideal for use in rivers and creeks along the Inland Passage; their slim hulls facilitated going far inland upriver against the current; and under sail they were to some degree seaworthy. Bryan's familiarity with such boats is well established, and early in the journal he called attention to a cypress swamp with trees up to six feet in diameter "as fine for Building canoos as any in this part of the world."[35]

Although he never explained the ultimate purpose of his journey, Bryan's main focus was on the land. Indeed, it seems that "land fever" was contagious in colonial Georgia. Most of the individuals he mentioned, some of whom owned thousands of acres, still actively sought to acquire even more. During the period 1753–1756 Bryan himself was heavily involved in land transactions, and through grants and purchases he added more than 18,000 acres to the tracts he already owned.

Bryan's journal also incorporates some assessment of Georgia's coastal fortifications that were once deemed essential for protection against Spanish and Indian intrusions but that by 1753 were in a deplorable state.[36] Certainly, his use of the colony's scout boat and armed men suggests an undertaking that had at least a quasi-official status even though minutes of the proceedings of the Georgia President and Assistants in Council make no mention of his journey.

In his observations of the islands, waterways, and adjacent mainland, Bryan noted particularly the vast timber resources and conditions suitable for settlement, livestock, and agriculture. He reflected an eighteenth-century viewpoint when he wrote, "I Thought it a great pitty such fine Lands should be uncultivated, when fertility, fine Timber and pleasant Situation promise ample reward to its future possessors." Then later, "what a Pity so much pleasant good land should lie uninhabited." Two-and-a-half centuries ago such perceptions were not contradictory—an unsettled wilderness was considered unsafe and wasteful, and overcrowding, pollution, and diminishing resources were unimagined.[37] From the beginning, Trustees of the Georgia colony accepted applications from persecuted European Protestants such as the Vaudois from Italy, Swiss Grisons, and the Salzburgers and Moravians from western Germany (only suspected Papists and Jews were turned away).[38] As a devout evangelical, Bryan saw the wilderness also as a "receptacle" for these persecuted Protestant congregations.

Throughout his journal Bryan demonstrated that not only was he observant and literate, but also that he appreciated the charm of poetry, twice (journal pages 19, 25) artfully placing verse into his account. His tribute to St. Catherines Island reads: "Here the spreading Oaks invite the Southern Breeze and rising Bars repel the foaming Seas, the Cristial Stream in winding rills proceed the rising Mounts and flow the Verdant Meads." Both of his selections, whether original or not, are heroic couplets, written in the iambic pentameter popular in his day.[39]

Bryan found the coastal region ideally suited for raising livestock; for cultivating rice, corn, oranges, and indigo; and for taking advantage of the fish abundant in surrounding waters. Some comments, therefore, about the area's agricultural development may be useful as background to his journal.

At the very beginning of the contact period in the sixteenth century, Spanish explorers and settlers introduced livestock from Iberia, the Atlantic Islands, and the Caribbean. This domestic stock soon roamed beyond Spanish settlements, generally adapting with ease to North America's more temperate zones. Following the arrival of South Carolina colonists, Indians who had traded deerskins for English goods learned that trading cattle was also to their advantage; the colonists in turn discovered that one of their most important exports, particularly to the West Indies, was beef. *Criollo* cattle were often small and scrubby looking but were hardier than British livestock.[40]

As it turned out, raising cattle, horses, and hogs became a valuable adjunct to sea island life. Cowpens were isolated mainland farmsteads with cattle pens, dwellings, and fields amidst large expanses of unfenced range. By contrast, the sea islands offered several advantages to stock raising. A sizable portion of Georgia's barrier islands consists of marshlands that fringe the inland navigation. Because of the water's high salinity certain areas on these marginal lands were unsuitable for cultivating crops, but the luxuriant carpet of grasses and rushes served as excellent grazing range for cattle. Colonial laws were almost uniform in requiring that crops be fenced to keep cattle

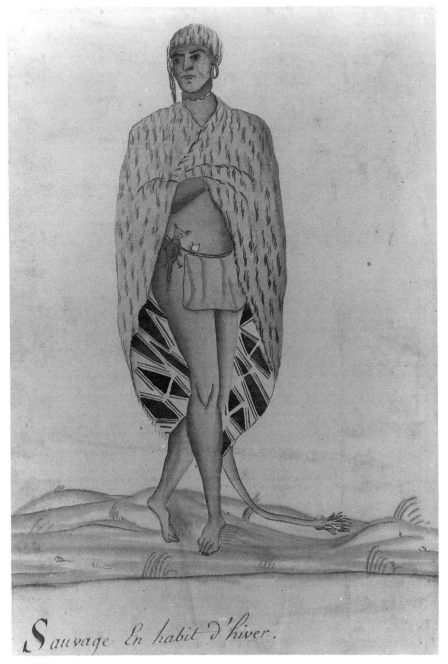

Sauvage En habit d'hiver.

*Drawing of a Southeastern Indian wearing a bison skin cloak
with painted geometric designs on the inside. Notice the tail. The artist has probably
drawn this cloak inside out since fur pelts and hides were customarily worn next to the skin.*

Engraving of a bison in Georgia, ca. *1740s*

out, which meant that open-range grazing was relatively easily achieved on the islands. The danger of theft was reduced given the natural and easy-to-control limits of islands, and in addition, sea and marsh afforded the most effective natural barriers to protect the herds from predators. Thus natural increase could proceed without interruption.[41]

Early settlers in Georgia cultivated their own crops including corn, wheat, potatoes, and peas, but corn initially was by far the most important. It is "the only cereal . . . which cannot reproduce itself without the aid of man" and is lauded for being the "most valuable food plant" native to the New World.[42] Lacking plows and draft animals, but armed with axe, hoe, and spade, most of Georgia's settlers could clear a little land to grow corn even in rough fields amid tree stumps, and this approach was far more practical and easier than trying to produce small grain such as wheat.[43] For this reason, beginning in the seventeenth century, corn became the staple food crop in America, and many consumed it in one form or another three times a day.[44] But it was not trouble-free: "[Either] the Drought burns or Rain drowns the Corn, and makes the Peas fall out of the Pod; Deer, which no Fences can exclude, devour those Little settlements in a night; Rats and squirrels do the same; Birds eat the seed out of the Ground, and dig up the Blade after it is Spired; and Variety of Worms and Insects devour the half of it."[45]

Rice was probably new to many of the early Georgia colonists, but within a year of their arrival in 1732/1733 they had a successful harvest from seed donated by South Carolina's general assembly. Gaining prominence in the eighteenth century, rice became the important staple food crop along the coast, and colonials consumed it daily in lieu of bread.[46] Its cultivation required intensive labor "in the muck of swamps," where intense heat, malaria, the threat of snakebite, and "the putrid and unwholesome effluvia from an oozy bottom and stagnated water poison[ed] the atmosphere."[47] Envious of slave labor on thriving South Carolina plantations, many settlers insisted that working conditions were too rigorous and unhealthy for English settlers to cultivate rice. Lifting the ban on slave labor, together with repealing restrictions on land tenure, resulted in a steady gain in rice culture along the Georgia coast.[48]

Early settlers planted rice on the inland river flood plains, but they had little control over the water supply. As planters gained knowledge about tidal action, "they adopted the practice of relying on tidal dynamics to flood rice fields, . . . [an] ingenious adaptation to nature . . . without parallel elsewhere on the continent" of North America. Two conditions were essential—"sufficient tidal range (3–7 feet) to facilitate field flooding . . . and a strong layering of fresh water to prevent saline water from entering the rice fields."[49]

Transforming swamps into productive rice fields required a prodigious amount of labor. Once temporary ditches and embankments were made around the designated swamp, it was drained. Removing debris, forming permanent embankments, installing trunks and sluice gates to control flooding and drain the fields, cutting channels across fields to facilitate drainage, and constructing cross banks to delineate each new field and contain the water when needed were just the beginning. They were followed by planting, cultivating, harvesting, and preparing the rice for market. Maintenance for the slaves and buying their implements were part of the cost. Rice production required more labor and a higher degree of technical supervision than any other antebellum agricultural endeavor.[50] About the time Bryan made his journey along the barrier islands, would-be planters were petitioning for land along the Savannah and Ogeechee River tidal marshes and adjacent tidal swamplands. In large measure their interest can be attributed to the combination of legalized slavery, more liberal land ownership laws, and an interval of international peace.[51] The river planters who managed to acquire hundreds of acres and obtain sufficient credit to initiate rice-growing operations evolved into a class that "began to resemble feudal estates, and their owners assumed the dignity and social bearing customary among men of such means."[52]

The ideal of establishing a closely settled colony led the Georgia promoters to aim at an economic system based largely on tropical or semitropical plants requiring intensive cultivation. Although indigo seemed a leading possibility in the 1740s, they placed greater emphasis on silk, wine, cotton, hemp, flax, and medicinal plants, as well as nuts and tropical fruits such as oranges, peaches, figs, and olives. To promote these aims the Trustees established an experimental ten-acre garden at Savannah and lined the walks with orange trees, but neither soil nor climate was well suited for such plants. In his 1738 survey for the Trustees concerning conditions in Georgia, Secretary William Stephens admitted that while Savannah soil was good for all sorts of fruits and grain, "Oranges have not so universally thriven with us, as was expected, by Reason of some severe Blasts by frost in the Spring."[53]

Nevertheless, many British settlers tried orange propagation for home consumption and export, perhaps with the hope of competing with the Florida fruit being shipped to English buyers as early as 1717.[54] (Charleston merchant Robert Pringle, for instance, shipped gallons of orange juice along with bags of dried orange peel from Frederica to London during 1746.) In addition to the popularity of orange juice in possets and other beverages, it was a favorite flavoring in pastries, stews, and

Detail from a 1757 map depicting slaves making indigo tablets for export

hashes; rind was candied; and syrup was made from the juice. Citrus juices were purported to have a number of beneficial effects, and although as late as 1795 the Royal Navy supplied such juices only on request, they were acknowledged as a cure for scurvy as early as 1747.[55]

Orange trees did not long survive in coastal Carolina or in Georgia without proper shelter, but it was not prolonged freezing weather that caused so much damage, because dormant trees are fairly hardy. The damage occurs when periods of high temperatures stir sap movements in the trees preceding cold snaps. Indeed, ruptured sap systems during a spring cold snap have killed more orange groves than any number of bitter winters. After a mild winter in South Carolina, an unexpected February frost in 1747 caused 300 orange trees to rupture. They were almost ready to blossom when the "Frost burst all their Vessels, for not only the Bark of all of them, but even the Bodies of many of them were split, and all on the Side next the Sun."[56] South Carolina exported over a quarter of a million oranges in 1747–1748; by the 1750s a limited market for citrus fruit extended to Georgia and Florida, but successful packaging of perishable fruit did not come about until the 1820s. Meanwhile, sudden spells of cold weather discouraged Georgia growers.[57]

Several times in his journal Bryan mentioned places with potential for growing indigo. This most popular of all vegetable dyes in the Colonial period yielded a range of rich blue hues and was sufficiently stable to withstand exposure to sunlight, boiling water, and strong soap—truly "in a class by itself."[58] Some of the best varieties thrived in the West Indies and Central America; in 1740 botanist Robert Miller suggested to the Trustees that it be produced in Georgia. It is easy to grow, but extracting good quality dye is a complex process, and early efforts in the southern colonies failed due to lack of experience. Eliza (Lucas) Pinckney in South Carolina is often credited with being the first to produce indigo dye that was praised by London merchants in 1742.[59]

Although planters considered rice cultivation without slaves too fatiguing for English settlers, planting indigo and producing the dye for export were deemed a suitable enterprise for both small-scale farmers and large plantations. On the other hand there was an obvious disadvantage: Vapors from the large malodorous vats of urea, filled with macerated leaves and branches from the plant, had a debilitating effect on people and were an attractive nuisance to certain insects. When the rice market plummeted in 1744 during King George's War, indigo gained importance; four years later the British Parliament encouraged production by establishing a premium or bounty on the dye regardless of quality. The heyday of indigo lasted only about thirty years, until the advent of the American Revolution, but in 1753 it was an increasingly significant commercial crop on the coasts of South Carolina and Georgia.[60]

Seemingly, Jonathan Bryan's journal emphasizes his interest in the Sea Islands. But he was looking ahead to a far more ambitious concern—penetration of the interior of Georgia and north Florida. Utilization of southeast Georgia's watercourses would bring about an extensive trade in rice, pitch, tar, turpentine, hemp, indigo, masts, pine, cypress, lumber of all sorts, Indian corn and "pease," and livestock. So also thought Charleston financiers in 1767, pleased to learn that Bryan intended to open up settlement on the lower Altamaha River. Henry Laurens, merchant and broker, immediately suggested expediting a customshouse at Frederica and establishing beacons and pilots on St. Simons and Jekyll Islands. Not only did the Altamaha provide water transport to the coast, but the Upper Altamaha was one of the terminals of the Alachua Trail. This centuries-old path crossed the almost-level watershed between the St. Johns and St. Marys Rivers, leading from the Alachua Savanna of Spanish Florida to the open and easily traversed pine barrens of southeastern Georgia. Ever since the withering of Spanish settlements, *criollo* livestock had followed this route to the upper Altamaha. Even though Frederica failed ultimately to become the entrepôt for south Georgia, it owed much of its shortlived success to the Alachua Trail.

Bryan's interest in the southern lands never abated, and he used his friendly relationship with the Creeks to good advantage. In 1773 Bryan and several associates were to secure a ninety-nine-year lease from the Creeks for the Apalachee Old Fields, an estimated 5 million acres of land in East Florida, bordered on its east by the St. Marys River. The validity of Bryan's compact was questioned in 1774 by Georgia's Gov. James Wright, and the outbreak of war in 1775 prevented Bryan from doing anything further with the Florida land. But it is clear that he saw south Georgia's great rivers as conduits of trade for the Florida hinterland, their mouths and sounds guarded by the southern barrier islands. It was also quite natural for Bryan to perceive the islands as staging areas for prosperous ports. Furthermore, only the barrier islands could furnish secure beacons and pilotage for incoming ocean-going vessels. In addition, passage through the barrier inlets provided security from bad weather; if adequately fortified, these islands would help repel attacks on shipping. And the abundance of excellent timber was ideal for constructing buildings as well as ships. Bryan saw the coastal islands in relationship to Georgia's rich interior—as guardians of the prospective settlement and trade that he so ardently admired.

Here, then, is the journal of a visionary.

The Journal

[The Journal]

onday the Sixth of August 1753. We left my Plantation at Indian Land in South Carolina, and arrived at my Plantation at Walnut-Hill in Georgia the next day about one of the Clock. the Day following we went to Savannah and waited on the President[61] and Council, who gave me an order for the Scout Boat commanded by Capt. Demetre[62] to attend us in our intended Voyage on our Discovery and Observations through the Colony of Georgia, and as far to the Southward as we should think proper to proceed. We set away from my landing in Georgia the 9th Aug. in company with Mr. William Simmons,[63] Capt. William De Brahm,[64] and Mr. John Williamson[65] to go to the Southward.

the next morning [10 August] at 6 o'Clock we passed through the Narrows a very difficult intricate passage. about noon we crossed great Ogeche [Ogeechee] River which runs up from Osseba [Ossabaw] Inlet, this is a bold fine River and runs some hundreds of miles up into the Country on the South side of the River, and the lowermost Point of the main Land; about Fifteen Miles from the Sea is a convenient Place to Settle a Town but not central enough for the capital of the Colony.[66] up this River is abundance of fine Land for Rice, corn and Indigo. this River is Subject to Inundation and has abundance of fresh Marsh and fine River Land, here lately several considerable Planters have begun to Settle. This afternoon we met with a smart Thunder Squall but secured our Selves from its violence by running into a small Creek. in the Evening we crossed St. Catharine's Sound and got to Mr. Bosomworth's[67] about Eight at night.

Mr. Adam Bosomworth[68] entertained us very kindly, and the next day being the Eleventh Instant We took a Tour across the Island on foot to view it. this Island is one of the most pleasant and agreeable Place[s] in all Georgia, it is in Length about Eighteen Miles and three or four Miles Broad, and seperated from the Main Land with Rivers & Marshes and distant from the Main about three Miles, the front is wash'd by the Sea and Banks very high Shaded by fine Spreading Live Oaks,[69] the middle of the Island appears a perfect Meadow being a large Savanna of about a Mile or Mile and half wide and four or five Miles long, and finely water'd with Springs.

this Island with a little Improvement would make one of the finest Seats for a Man of Fortune, in all Georgia. Here Spreading Oaks invite the Southern Breeze and rising Bar [sandbar] repel the foaming Seas, the cristial [crystal] Streams in winding rills proceeds the rising Mounts and flow the verdant meads. after about three Hours

Walk we return'd with a fine young Buck which gave us good diversion on the Sea Beech with Mr. Bosomworth's Hounds. This Evening we proceeded up Newport River, and arrived at the Head about thirty five or fforty [*sic*] Miles upon Mr. Simmons intended Land.[70] We went on sho[re] and encamped on a fine Hill about a Quarter of a Mile from the River.

August 12 [Sunday]. about 12 oClock. here seems to be a very large Quantity of good Rice, corn and Indigo land, the head of this River makes a very fine cypress Swam[p] many of the Trees of a very large Size from thr[ee], four, to five and Six foot through and Sixty, seventy foot without limbs, perhaps as fine for Building canoos as any in this part of the world. I thought it [a] great pitty such fine Lands should be uncultivated, when fertility, fine Timber and pleasant Situation promis[es] ample reward to its future Possessors. Here the Weather came on very bad and rainy which prevented our penetrating so far into the Woods as we intended.

On Monday morning [13 August] Mr. Simmons began to clear Land for a new Settlement with Sixteen hands, which he brought up with him for that Purpose. I hope his Example and good Success may be an Encouragement to many others to engage in the Settlement of these valuable Lands. Last Night I could not help reflecting on the Special Providence of Almighty God, who has cast out so many Thousands of the Heathen before us, who were but a few years ago the numerous Inhabitants of these desolate Places so that it is now a rare thing to see the Face of an Indian in any of these parts, perhaps these Lands are designed as a receptacle for the Professors of his Glorious Gospel and persecuted church in some parts of Europe.

Tuesday Morning [14 August] Mr. Simmons began his Survey, but was prevented by bad Weather. Wednesday [15 August] we ended the Survey of Mr. Simmons Land, and observed that there was a goo[d] Body of Land lying above his one thousand acres, part of which was fine cypress and Tupelo, Swamp and good corn land adjoining. here is room both above and below Mr. Simmons Land for

[*An unknown number of leaves are missing here for part of Wednesday through part of Saturday, 16–18 August.*][71]

part of his own Stock prepar'd for his Voyage to Carolina, but however ill he could spare these Provisions, he parted with them with very freely, and were very acceptable in this place. we parted about 5 o'Clock, and proceeded up the River, which seperates Sapelo Island from the Main. Sapelo River, which leads into the Main is a short River and soon loses itself in small Branches, on these Branches are good Land. here the two Mackintosh's[72] and some others are Setled (this I had by Information).

Live oak foliage (Quercus virginiana)

This afternoon we had a very agreeable View of the Island of Sapelo, the rising Banks covered with Green Grass with the evergreen Trees along the Banks, which looks as if they were shorn and made even by Art, afforded a very Pleasant Prospect. on this Island about a Mile from the North End is the remains of an old Spanish Fort,[73] in a pleasant green Field. here is also a very pleasant Mount, with a fine running Stream of water at its foot [?]. this Island is a most agreeable Spot, with fine Land for Corn or Indigo, and would admit or [sic] eight or ten good Settlements. we turned into a Creek called Tea-Kettle Creek which leads to Doboy Inlet, and lay by all Night in a small Creek about a Mile or two from the Inlet; observed the South End of Sapelo to be much broken with Creeks and entirely divide[d] into two seperates [sic] Islands, which are distinguished by great Sapelo and little Sapelo. these Islands are about fourteen miles long and very good for Stock.

about half an Hour after five this Morning being Sunday [19 August] we enter'd Doboy Sound, which is a very poor Inlet, with reefs of Sands running clear across, and a small Island to the South of the Inlet called Wolf Island. Doby [sic] Island is a little Hammock of about ten Acres, about a Mile above the Inlet it appears perfectly round. this Island is a fine mark in the Night to cross the Sound by. we entered Doboy Creek about half an Hour after Six and passed into the North mouth of the Alatamahaw [Altamaha] River, about a Quarter afte[r] Seven. We entered Mud River, which leads into the main Stream of the Alatamahaw River, and both vent into Egg Island Sound on the South Side of Wolf Island. Egg Island is a small Sandy Island, with a few Trees on it, and lies in the middle of the Sound so that these two Inlets of Doboy and Egg Island, make one large Sound only parted by Wolf Island, which is a small kind of a Hammock not above thirty or forty acres of Land. the Main Stream of the Alatamahaw falls into the Sea between Egg Island and the North End of little St. Simons.

we then proceeded up the main stream of the Alatamahaw, this is a fine bold fresh River which vents itself into three mouths, the North Mouth into Doboy Sound, the Main or middle Stream into Egg Island sound, and the South into Jekyll Sound[74] to the Southward of great St. Simons. the general course into the Main is N.W. 70 it runs up into the Country several hundred Miles to the Indian Nations, the lower part of the River being divided into several Streams, makes a good many Islands, and a vast Quantity of River Swamps and fresh Marsh; up this River is abundance of fine Rice Land, where might be made great Quantities of Rice and very convenient for Exportation from Frederica,[75] a Port in the South Mouth of the same River capable to receive Vessels of any Burthen.

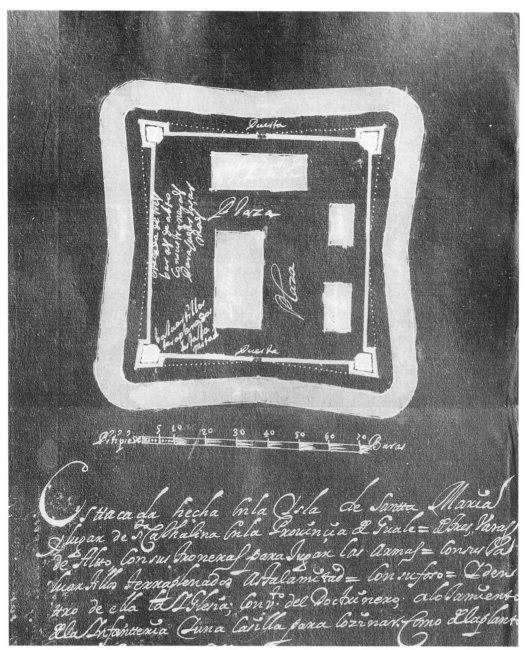

Plan of Mission Santa Catalina de Guale on Amelia Island, Florida, drawn ca. *1691*

about twenty Miles above Frederica on the North Side of the River is the Scotch Settlement called Darian [Darien].[76] at about two hundred Miles up, the River divides into two Branches, one of which is called the Occones [Oconee] the other Ockmulges [Ockmulgee]; this River is subject to great Freshes [freshets],[77] as described in Savanna, and almost as large a River. the N.E. Branch which is called Occones almost joins with a Branch of Savanna call'd broad River. they both disperse and loose themselves in the Mountains, and on these Branches lie a great Quantity of good Land. I have been well informed that the most of the Land which lies between this River and great St. tille River [now Satilla] is a fine Body of good Land, and room for some hundreds of Inhabitants.

We came down the South Stream of the River and got to one Abbotts[78] on the N.W. Point of great St. Simons about 12 o'Clock. here we stopt a while, and about two we got to Frederica. This Town was built & fortified round by General Oglethorpe, with regular Bastions and a Citadel towards the River, with Spur work and a good Number of large Cannon and Mortars, but now it is all in ruins, the Stores Mazaunes [magazines] and many good Tabby Buildings, all in a ruinous Condition, the Melancholy Prospect of Houses without Inhabitants, Barracks without Soldiers, Guns without Carriages and the Streets grown over with Weeds, appeared to me with a very horrible Aspect, and so very different from what I once knew it, that I could scarce refrain from Tears.

this Place of so great Importance [to] the Frontier of his Majestys Dominions on the Continent, so convenient for Ships of War, and might be made the Key of the Bahama Straights and Gulf of Florida, and was once the Means of preserving both the Colonys of Carolina and Georgia, in that memorable Defeat given the Spaniards of [by] General Oglethorpe in their intended Invasion of these Parts, with no less than thirty five Sail of Vessels, and upwards of four thousand Men. this valuable and important Place totally neglected since the disbanding of General Oglethorpes Troops, Seven hundred of which were quartered in and about this Town. the breaking of his Regiment, the two Companys of Rangers and other Extra Companys, has been the sole cause of this Place's declining and sinking into Contempt and almost nothing. the poor Inhabitants whose Industry were encouraged, Familys Supported and Property defended by the Regiment, are quite dispirited, and mostly removed quite away, and left their Habitations, being afraid to expose themselves and Familys to the Insults of their troublesom Neighbours the Spaniards.

O Frederica! had thy Founder known,
The Calamitous Days that were to come,
Or had thy Genius let thy Builder see,
The secret purpose of Divine Decree,
How soon thy walls defenceless should remain,
And those lofty Towers level'd to the Plain,
Thy Bastions once, whose Cannon thundered o'er,
To Neighbouring Spain, and F[l]orida a Law
To be disdain'd, not worthy Britain's Care,
Had caus'd a Sigh, and forc'd a briny Tear.

Capt. Demere[79] has a company [with] about Fifty Men for this Place, but they were either out on Detachments or upon Furloughs, so that there was not as I was informed above twelve Men in the Town at this Time of my being there.

the few Inhabitants of the Town, particularly Capt. Demetre and Mr. Penny,[80] a Serjeant of Capt. Demetre's Company, us'd us very kindly. we had Fruit & Punch[81] in great Plenty and the Town appears a perfect Grove, with the Orange Trees[82] laden with Fruit, and a fine Grove of Shady Oaks which lie to the Southward, adds exceedingly to the Prospect of this agreeable Spot, and might be improved by a little art and Industry into a most delightful place. here are as great Plenty of Fish as ever I saw, which are a great help to the poor remaining Inhabitants.

I shew'd Capt. Demetre the President's order for the Scout Boat to accompany us to the Southward, as we were not certain, but there might be some danger in approaching so near the Spaniards in a defenceless Condition. in a little Time Capt. Demetre got his Boat ready clean'd, with two Swivel Guns on her Bow, and ten clever hearty Fellows double armed, which with our own Boat, we thought sufficient to oppose any thing we should meet with in St. Johns River.

Tuesday [21 August] about 3 in the morning we left Frederica, and went down to St. Simons Point, about ten Miles below Frederica, where was formerly a Battery of ten or twelve Pieces of cannon to secure the Inlet. this Place is now quite defence-less, and the cannon almost buried in the Sand.[83] Capt. Demetre and his People at low Water took more Fresh Fish then served us all for Dinner, tho' we were in both Boats twenty two in Number. We took the Flood [tide], and went up to the middle of Jekyl[l] Island. We went a Shore to wait for the Tide. Capt. Demetre again took a good Quantity of Fish.

Mr. Simons and I went up to see Major Horton's[84] Plantations and Buildings at Jekyl. I was Surprizd at the extraordinary Expense this Gentleman must have been at

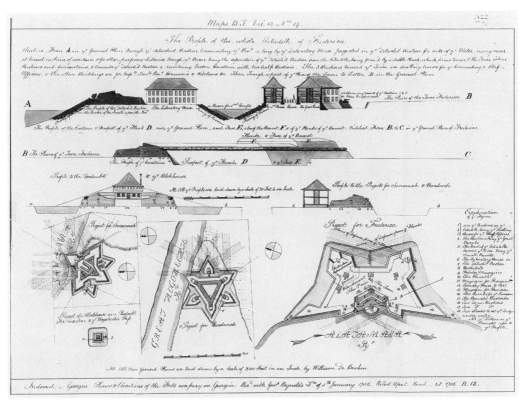

Elevation for an improved Fort Frederica from William De Brahm's plans, ca. 1754, which he submitted to Governor John Reynolds

in the Setling and improving of this Place. he has a handsome dwelling house of about forty foot long by twenty wide, neatly finish'd and Glazed, a good House for his Overseer about thirty by twenty, a Malt House of Eighty or one hundred foot long by thirty, all these of Tabby, also a large Brew-house of wood with all Conveniencies for Brewing, a large Barn and Stables and other Conveniences too numerous to mention; he has a large Orange Garden, now loaded with Fruit, a good Stock of about three hundred Head of Cattle and one hundred Head of Horses.[85] This Place is about ten Miles from Frederica; the Island is about nine Miles long and two Miles wide it is very fit for Stock and some good planting Land on it. there is now only a Soldier to take care of the Buildings.

Past the Mouth of Carrs River, which vents into Jekyl Sound. up this River Capt Carr[86] was Setled, and had fine improvements, but are now all deserted and in Ruins. there is a Neck of fine Land lying between this River and the South of the Alatamahaw and at a Place called the White Post,[87] on this neck of Land opposite to the Town of Frederica, used to be posted a Guard of Rangers which always on any alarm or approach of the Enemy Indians gave a Signal to the Town by a Smoke.

after Dinner we set away and got to St. Andrews Sound about 3 o'clock. This is a fine large Sound and a pretty good Bar to enter here is about twelve foot water at low water; this Inlet Parts Jekyl and Cumberland Islands. We went up the River St. Tillet whose Course into the Main bears about W.N.W. from the Sound. about two miles up a Creek[88] which leads to the South Point of the Main and makes a fine Bluff, and the Land seems to be good planting Land. we lay by about four Miles up the River, and in the Morning [22 August] we went up the River, observed a large Branch turn to the Northward about ten Miles up from the Sound. this Branch by its appearance runs a good way into the Main, and must Vent some large swamps by the water being so fresh. we kept the Main Stream of the River, and landed about Sixteen Miles up on a fine clay Bluff. this Bluff is about twenty foot above high water mark, and above a Mile long, and on the South side of the River here the River is fine and fresh, the Marsh to the opposite Shore about a mile wide, here we Dined on some excellent Fish. I can't but believe there is a great Quantity of good Land up the River, as the Land appears very high and a Clay Soil. We were informed by our Pilot that there is several Bluffs on the River higher up, and abundance of good Oak and cedar Timber.

Capt. Carr had a trading House about Seventy miles up, and the River runs a very considerable way up higher than this trading House; on the South Side of this River are abundance of wild cattle, which have stray'd from the old Spanish Settlements, and the Apalache Old Fields. here the Creek Indians are almost always a hunting for Cattle, Deer, and Buffalo.[89] I have been inform'd by some Hunters that used this River that there is large Quantity of white oak and fine Cane Swamps, and am of opinion from all that I could see, and learn from others, that here is room for a great number of Familys to Settle.

We set away about half an hour after three, and fell down the River to the sound. at Night we lay by in a Creek. in the Morning [23 August] went down the Sound to Cumberland Island, this is a fine high Island about twenty two Miles long, and three or four Miles wide, it is Separated from the Main by Rivers and Marshes, about two or three Miles distant from the Main Land. On this Island General Oglethorpe, built a Fort, about two miles from the North End to secure the Inland Passage,[90] and two of the companies belonging to the Regiment were lodged there, and a good many of the Soldiers who had Familys were settled in a Village[91] on the Side of a Creek, which runs into the Island. and towards the South End of the Island, were Setled above twenty Familys whose Plantations are now all deserted and left desolate, so that there is not an Inhabitant on the Island, only a Corporal and Six Men that resides on the South End in Fort William.[92] We went ashore at St. Andrews Fort,[93] which is now all ruins, where were two Hunters who supply'd us with Bears Flesh and Venison. this Morning Capt. Demetre took again a good Parcel of Fish.

We then proceeded to the Southward up the River, which seperates Cumberland from the Main, but Mr. De Brahm, who had been ailing two or three days and seem'd quite dispirited desired to return, as he thought his proceeding farther would endanger his Life, upon which we order'd my Boat & Hands to carry him back to Frederica, then Mr. Simmons, John Williamson and myself, went on Board Capt. Demetre's Boat, and so proceeded up the River to the main. here is a poor low Scrubby Land good for little. at twelve o'Clock a very hard Thunder Squall overtook us, which lasted about half or three Quarters of an Hour. We came to the Mouth of the River called the dividing River,[94] but by the Indians Slafea-Gufea,[95] it runs up about twenty or thirty Miles into the Main, and is noted for the fine Cedar which grows there, great Quantities of which have been cut for the building of Fort William.

about 4 oClock we turn'd the point of Main Land on the North of St. Maries [St. Marys], we went up a Creek which makes a Bluff on this Point of Land. here we went ashore, and from this Bluff we had a prospect of Fort William, which bears S.E. 80. St. Maries River vents its Self into Amelia Inlet, between the South End of Cumberland and the North End of Amelia Island. It is a Large Fresh River, and runs up a very considerable way into the Main, it makes a very fine Bluff. on the South Side about ten Miles up the Bluff appears as high as the Bluff at Savannah, from whence you have a view of the Inlet and Fort William. We were informed by a Person who had been four days row up the River that there were several fine Bluffs upwards, and that there was the greatest Quantity of fine Cedar that he had seen, the trees in common twenty or thirty foot without Limbs, and from a foot to Eighteen Inches through. that on the Sides of the River was fine Swamps for Rice, and the High Lands very full of white oak for Staves. The Lands on and near the head of this River is very open and Grassy (so that a Person may see Miles before him, only here and there a Hill of oak land) with fine Springs of water. These Lands are full of wild cattle and Buffalo. This is the last River in Georgia, and the next River to St. John's River.

Friday August 24th in the Morning we went down to view Fort William, which is Situated on the North Side of Amelia Inlet, on the very South Point of Cumberland Island. It was laid out by Collo. [Col.] Cook[96] and was one of the compleatest pieces of Fortification in any of these parts (tho' small) and used to contain, before the Regiment was broke, a Fort Major, and Fifty men to defend it. it was attacked by the Spaniards with Seventeen small vessels (viz) Gallys[97] Shorebacks[98] and Settees[99] and one thousand Men, at the Time of the Spanish Invasion, and bravely defended by the commanding officer and thirty two men. I saw some of the Shot Holes which had penetrated through the Tower from the nine Pounders on Board the Gallys. the Tower being of wood the Splinters wounded some of the Soldiers, which was the only damage they received in four Hours attack. This Place of defence was greatly damaged by the last Hurricane,[100] and in a ruinous Condition, and now quite neglected, as all the other Fortifications are throughout Georgia. I wish we may not sooner than we expect, find our great Loss in the neglect of these Places of so much Consequence to our Safety, there is now in this ruin'd Fort only a Corporal and Six Men.

Here came on a violent Storm of Wind at NE and Rain which came on the Night before, but now with greater Violence, which prevented our going over the Sound to Amelia, which is the next Island to the Southward of Cumberland, and is a very pleasant Island about twenty four miles long and three or four miles wide. this Island was formerly inhabited by Spaniards who had setled and well improved it by clearing several Plantations and building some good Buildings. the ruins of one large Brick Building[101] is yet to be seen. here are a Grove of Orange Trees supposed to be standing ever since the Spaniards lived here who were dispossessed and driven of [off] by General Moor [Moore][102] about Fifty years ago, and ever since the Island has lain vacant, only General Oglethorpe built a small Fort on it, mounting four Pieces of

Drawing of a multilevel fortification from the notebooks of Philip von Reck. Notice the tents. This is almost certainly Fort St. Andrews, Cumberland Island. The cannon arrived on 2 May 1736, and the stockade was complete when von Reck visited three weeks later on 23 May.

cannon, to guard the pass at the North End.[103] what a Pity so much pleasant good land should lie uninhabited.

To the Southward of this Island, is yet another Sea Island call'd Talbot Island[104] this is the last Island in the front of Georgia. the great River of St. John's vents its self by the South End of this Island. and just above this Island of Talbot, betwext it and the Main and on the North Side of St. John's River, lies another little Island called St. Georges Island.[105] here the General built his last fort, by which he intended to secure both the Passes. the Pass up St. John's River, and a back passage which leads from the North End of Talbot into St. John's River, but after he had built the Fort and placed a command in it, he again withdrew the command and demolished the Fort, but for what Reason I never knew, perhaps he thought it too distant from the Main Body of his Troops to be supported.

This afternoon we set away from Fort William homeward, the bad Weather continuing, and at Night a terrible Storm came on. we came to an anchor, and lay all night, hoping to cross Cumberland Sound in the Morning, but the Weather continued. our poor Men Suffer'd very much, being obliged to endure all the Hardship of Wind and Weather, and not the least Shelter, and not a dry Ragg for two or three days past. We went into a Creek below St. Andrews and went ashore. our People made a large Fire and dried themselves. at St. Andrews a Hunter gave us two fine fat Does, and one of our own Men shot a Buck, which as it was difficult to get it to the Boat, we left behind. here our People feasted on Venison and Raccons the latter of which they seem to prefer to any kind of Flesh whatever. The Rain ceased and we proceeded over the Sound. here we were in a good deal of danger, the Wind being very hard and forward of the Beam, and a great Sea, when we had got about half over, we were obliged to bear away before it into a Creek at the Head of the Sound. and (I thank Almighty God) with difficulty got out of danger, we proceeded till Night which coming on very dark, we lay by in Jekyl Creek, till 3 oClock, then crossed Jekyl Sound, and got up to Frederica Sunday morning being the 26th August. Here we found Capt. De Brahm almost recover'ed of his Illness.

On Monday Morning the 27th of August, we set away from Frederica, we had a fine Wind, and in the Evening we got to St. Catherine's. the Weather being rainy and dark, we lay at Mr. Bosomworth's all Night. in the Morning [28 August] we crossed St. Catherine's Sound, here we had a fine view of Capt. Carrs intended Town, which has the finest Prospect to the Sea imaginable, and all the advantages of Situation, being in the Center of the colony, and contigious [contiguous] to a vast Quantity of good Lands, which are now Setling very fast.[106] the only objection against its being a Place of very considerable Trade may be the want of Sufficient water for

Alligator, some acorns, and a coral snake,
drawn by a visitor to Georgia in the early 1730s

His unfinished drawing of a skimmer

Ships of Burthen, tho' the Barr is very good, yet, I am informed, there is not more than ten foot Water in the River in one place at low Water. to Day we pass'd by Ossebaw Island. I have been over this Island, and observe it to be very much broken with Creeks and Marshes, with several low brackish Savannas, and no large Quantity of good planting Land in any one Place. I believe it is about twelve or ffourteen [*sic*] Miles long on the Sea Shore. We called at Green Island[107] at Mr. James Maxwells,[108] and dine'd with his two Sons and Daughter, who entertain'd us kindly, he and Mrs. Maxwell were gone to Midway where he is Settling a new Plantation. this is a pleasant Spot on the Bank of Vernon River.[109] Mr. Maxwell has a fine Orange Garden, and a pleasant little House, tho too small for his Family, and Conveniences about him. In the Evening we passed the narrows and got home again to my House next Morning, being the 29th August 1753.

In Georgia are fourteen Rivers, which leads into the Main, twelve Sea Islands, and thirteen Inland Islands, which lie between the Sea Islands and the Main[110]

The names of these Rivers

1 Savanna a fresh River 250 M [miles] to Augusta
2 Vernon
3 little Ogeehee [Ogeechee]
4 Great Ogeehee, fresh, some hundred Miles up
5 Midway
6 Newport, 40 miles long
7 South Newport
8 Sapelo
9 Alatamahaw [Altamaha], fresh 70 miles from Savannah
10 Carrs River
11 Little St. Tillee [Little Satilla]
12 Great St. Tillee, fresh
13 Dividing or SlepaGufea [*sic*]
14 St. Marie's [St. Marys], fresh

[*Notation on the inside cover in a different hand:*]
Journal to and a Description of Georgia, especially of the Islands of St. Catharine, Osseba & Sappalo, of Which three islands I Levy owned a moiety.

Short Titles, Abbreviations, and Location Symbols

Abbot, *Royal Governors*
> Abbot, W. W. *The Royal Governors of Georgia, 1754–1775.* Chapel Hill: University of North Carolina Press, 1959.

Alford, "Boat Building"
> Alford, Michael B. "French Boat Building in the Carolina Colonies." Museum Small Craft Association, *19th Annual Conference Proceedings.* Thibodeaux LA: Center for Traditional Louisiana Boat Building, Nicholls State University, 1992.

Alford, "S.C. Vessel Types"
> Alford, Michael B., and Mark Newell. "South Carolina Vessel Types." Museum Small Craft Association, *19th Annual Conference Proceedings, Oct. 9, 10, 11, 1992.* Thibodeaux LA: Center for Traditional Louisiana Boat Building, Nicholls State University, 1992.

Abercromby Letter Book
> *The Letter Book of James Abercromby, Colonial Agent, 1751–1773.* Edited by John C. Van Horne and George Reese. Richmond: Virginia State Library and Archives, 1991.

Argyle Island
> *Life and Labor on Argyle Island: Letters and Documents of a Savannah River Rice Plantation, 1833–1867.* Edited by James M. Clifton. Savannah: Beehive Press, 1978.

Bailey, *Hortus Third*
> Bailey, Liberty Hyde, and Ethel Zoe Bailey, comp. Rev. ed. *Hortus Third: A Concise Dictionary of Plants Cultivated in the United States and Canada. . . .* New York: Macmillan, 1976.

Baine, "Creek Pictograph"
> Baine, Rodney M. "The Myth of the Creek Pictograph." *Atlanta History: A Journal of Georgia and the South* 32 (1988): 43-52.

"Barnwell's Journal"
> "Journal of Col. John Barnwell (Tuscarora) in the Construction of the Fort of the Altamaha in 1721. . . . " Edited by Joseph W. Barnwell. *SCHGM* 27 (1926):189-203.

Bartram, "Diary"
> Bartram, John. "Diary of a Journal Through the Carolinas, Georgia, and Florida, from July 1, 1765, to April 10, 1766." Annotated by Francis Harper. *Transactions of the American Philosophical Society* 33, pt. 1 (1942).

BDSC
> *Biographical Directory of the South Carolina House of Representatives. Volume II. The Commons House of Assembly, 1692–1775.* Edited by Walter B. Edgar and N. Louise Bailey. Columbia: University of South Carolina Press, 1977.

Blaitie, *Land Degradation*
> Blaitie, Piers, and Harold Brookfield. *Land Degradation and Society.* London: Mathuen, 1987.

Board of Trade
> *Journal of the Commissioners for Trade and Plantations . . . 1750 to . . . 1775 Preserved in the Public Record Office.* 14 vols. London: H.M. Stationery Office, 1920–1938.

Bonner, *Georgia Agriculture*
> Bonner, James C. *A History of Georgia Agriculture, 1732–1860.* Athens: University of Georgia Press, 1964.

Bryant, *English Crown Grants*
> Bryant, Pat. *English Crown Grants for Islands in Georgia, 1755–1775.* Atlanta: State of Georgia, 1972.

Buchanan, *Weaver's Garden*
> Buchanan, Rita. *A Weaver's Garden.* Loveland CO: Interweave Press, 1987.

Bullard, "Cumberland Island's Dungeness"
> Bullard, Mary R. "In Search of Cumberland Island's Dungeness: Its Origins and English Antecedents." *GHQ* 76 (1992): 67-86.

Bullard, *Robert Stafford*
> Bullard, Mary R. *Robert Stafford of Cumberland Island: Growth of a Planter.* DeLeon Springs FL: E. O. Painter Printing Co., 1986. Reprint, Athens: University of Georgia Press, 1995.

Calendar of State Papers
> *Calendar of State Papers. Colonial Series. America and West Indies Preserved in the Public Record Office . . . 1737.* 44 vols. Edited by K. G. Davies. London: H.M. Stationery Office, 1963.

Cashin, *Colonial Augusta*
> Cashin, Edward J. *Colonial Augusta "Key of the Indian Countrey."* Macon GA: Mercer University Press, 1986.

Catalogue of I. K. Tefft
> *Catalogue of the Entire Collection of Autographs of the late Mr. I. K. Tefft of Savannah, Georgia.* New York: Leavitt, Strebeigh & Co., [1867].

Cate Coll.
> Cate, Margaret Davis, Collection. Georgia Historical Society, Savannah.

Cate, "Fort Frederica"
> Cate, Margaret Davis. "Fort Frederica and the Battle of Bloody Marsh." *GHQ* 27 (1943): 111-74.

Cate, *Our Todays*
> Cate, Margaret Davis. *Our Todays and Yesterdays: A Story of Brunswick and the Coastal Islands.* Rev. ed. Brunswick GA: Glover Brothers, 1930. Reprint, Spartanburg SC: Reprint Co., 1972.

Catesby, *Natural History*
> Catesby, Mark. *Natural History of Carolina, Florida and the Bahama Islands. . . .* 2 vols. London: Printed for B. White, 1771.

CGHS
> *Collections of the Georgia Historical Society.*

Chesnutt, *South Carolina's Expansion*

 Chesnutt, David R. *South Carolina's Expansion Into Colonial Georgia, 1720–1765.* New York: Garland Publishing Co., 1986.

Clark, *Colonial Soldiers*

 Clark, Murtie June. *Colonial Soldiers of the South, 1732–1774.* Baltimore: Genealogical Publishing Co., 1983.

Cline, *Women's Diaries*

 Cline, Cheryl. *Women's Diaries, Journals, and Letters: An Annotated Bibliography.* New York: Garland Publishing, 1989.

Clute, *St. Thomas and St. Denis Parish*

 Clute, Robert F. *The Annals and Parish Register of St. Thomas and St. Denis Parish, in South Carolina, From 1680 To 1884.* Charleston SC: Walker, Evans & Cogswell, 1884. Reprint. Baltimore: Genealogical Publishing Co., 1974.

CMSA

 Colonial Museum & Savannah Advertiser.

Coldham, *American Loyalists Claims*

 Coldham, Peter Wilson. *American Loyalists Claims Abstracted from the Public Record Office Audit Office Series 13, Bundles 1-35 & 37.* Washington DC: National Genealogical Society, 1980.

Colonial Records of SC

 Colonial Records of South Carolina. The Journal of the Commons House of Assembly. 14 vols. Edited by J. H. Easterby. Columbia: Historical Commission of South Carolina, 1951–1989.

Colonial Wills

 Abstracts of Colonial Wills of the State of Georgia, 1733–1777. Compiled by Atlanta Town Committee, National Society, Colonial Dames of America in the State of Georgia for the Department of Archives and History. Hapeville GA: Longino & Porter, 1962.

Connolly, *Royal Engineers*

 Connolly, T. W. J., comp. *Roll of Officers of the Corps of Royal Engineers From 1660 To 1898.* Chatham: Royal Engineers Institute, 1898.

Conveyances C-1

 Beckemeyer, Frances Howell, comp. *Abstracts of Georgia Colonial Conveyance Book, C-1, 1750–1761.* Atlanta: R. J. Taylor, Jr., Foundation, 1975.

Conveyances J

 Walker, George F., comp. *Abstracts of Georgia Colonial Book J, 1755–1762.* Atlanta: R. J. Taylor, Jr., Foundation, 1978.

Cook, *Fort King George*

 Cook, Jeannine. *Fort King George: One Step to Statehood.* Darien GA: Printed by the Darien News, 1990.

Coon, "Market Agriculture"

 Coon, David L. "The Development of Market Agriculture in South Carolina, 1670–1785." Ph.D. diss., University of Illinois at Urbana-Champaign, 1972.

Corkran, *Creek Frontier*
    Corkran, David H. *The Creek Frontier, 1540–1783*. Norman: University of Oklahoma Press, 1976.

Coulter, *Georgia Waters*
    Coulter, E. Merton. *Georgia Waters: Tallulah Falls, Madison Springs, Scull Shoals and the Okefenokee Swamp*. Athens: Georgia Historical Quarterly, 1965.

Coulter, *Joseph Vallence Bevan*
    Coulter, E. Merton. *Joseph Vallence Bevan, Georgia's First Official Historian*. Athens: University of Georgia Press, 1964.

Council Journal, 1753–1760
    Georgia Governor and Council Journals, 1753–1760. Abstracted by Mary Bondurant Warren and Jack Moreland Jones. Danielsville GA: Heritage Papers, 1991.

Council Journal 1761–1767
    Georgia Governor and Council Journals, 1761–1767. Abstracted by Mary Bondurant Warren and Jack Moreland Jones. Athens GA: Heritage Papers, 1992.

Crane, *Southern Frontier*
    Crane, Verner W. *Southern Frontier, 1670–1732*. Durham NC, 1928. Reprint, New York: Norton, 1981.

CRG
    The Colonial Records of the State of Georgia. Vols. 1-19, 21-26. Edited by Allen D. Candler et al. Atlanta: State Printer, 1904–1916. Vols. 20, 27-32. Edited by Kenneth Coleman and Milton Ready. Athens: University of Georgia Press, 1976–1989.

Deagan, "Spanish-American Colonization"
    Deagan, Kathleen, "Sixteenth-Century Spanish-American Colonization in the Southeastern United States and the Caribbean," in *Columbian Consequences, Archaeological and Historical Perspectives on the Spanish Border*. Washington DC: Smithsonian Institution Press, 1991.

De Brahm, *History*
    De Brahm, J. G. W. *History of the Province of Georgia with Maps of Original Surveys*. Wormsloe [GA], 1849.

De Brahm, 1752 MS map
    A Map of Savannah River beginning at Stone-Bluff, or Nexttobethell, which continueth to the Sea; also, the Four Sounds Savanah, Hossabaw, and St: Katharines with their Islands likewise Newport, or Serpent River, from its mouth to Benjehova bluff. Surveyed by William Noble of Brahm late Captain Ingenier under his Imperial Majesty Charles the VII. Colored manuscript map, 1752, Faden Coll., No. 45, Geography and Map Division, DLC.

De Brahm, *Map* (1757)
    De Brahm, John Gerar William. *A map of South Carolina and a part of Georgia. Containing the whole sea-coast; all the islands, inlets, rivers, creeks, parishes, townships, borough, roads, and bridges; as also several plantations, with their proper boundary-lines, their names, and the names of their proprietors. Composed from surveys taken by the Hon. William Bull, Esq., Lieutenant Governor, Captain Gascoign, Hugh Bryan, Esq; and the author William De Brahm, surveyor*

general to the province of South Carolina, one of the surveyors of Georgia, and late captain engineer under His Imperial Majesty Charles VII. Engraved by Thomas Jefferys, geographer to His Royal Highness the Prince of Wales. London, 1757. Copy in the Geography and Map Division, DLC.

De Brahm, *Report*
De Brahm's Report of the General Survey in the Southern District of North America. Edited with an introduction by Louis De Vorsey, Jr. Columbia: University of South Carolina Press, 1971.

Demere Papers.
Demere, Raymond, Papers. William R. Perkins Library, Duke University, Durham NC.

De Vorsey, "Early Maps"
Louis De Vorsey, "Early Maps and the Land of Ayllón." In *Columbus and the Land of Ayllón: The Exploration and Settlement of the Southeast.* Edited by Jeannine Cook. Darien GA: Lower Altamaha Historical Society-Ayllon, 1992.

DGB
Dictionary of Georgia Biography. 2 vols. Athens: University of Georgia Press, 1983.

Dickinson's Journal
Jonathan Dickinson's Journal. Edited by Evangeline Walker Andrews and Charles McLean Andrews. New Haven: Yale University Press, 1945.

Disputed Ruins
Georgia's Disputed Ruins. Edited by E. Merton Coulter. Chapel Hill: University of North Carolina Press, 1937.

DLC
Library of Congress.

DNA
National Archives and Records Administration, Washington DC.

DNB
Dictionary of National Biography. 66 vols. London: Smith, Elder & Co., 1885–1901.

Downing, *Fruit Trees of America*
Downing, A. J. The Fruits and Fruit Trees of America. New York: Wiley & Putnam, 1845.

Dumont, *Colonial Georgia*
Dumont, William H. *Colonial Georgia Genealogical Data, 1748–1783.* Special Publication No. 36. Washington DC: National Genealogical Society, 1971.

"Dunlop's Voyage"
"Journall. Capt. Dunlop's Voyage to the Southward. 1687." *SCHGM* 30 (1929): 127-33.

Early Epitaphs
Some Early Epitaphs in Georgia. Compiled by the Georgia Society of the Colonial Dames of America, with a foreword and sketches by Mrs. Peter W. Meldrim. Durham NC, 1924.

Early Settlers
A List of the Early Settlers of Georgia. Edited by E. Merton Coulter and Albert B. Saye. Athens: University of Georgia Press, 1949. [See corrections and additions of Lilla M. Hawes and Margaret Davis Cate in Robert S. Davis, Jr., "Georgia's First Settlers; Revised, Corrected,

Annotated and Cross Referenced," *A Researcher's Library of Georgia History, Genealogy, and Records Sources.* Easley SC: Southern Historical Press, 1987.]

Egmont, *Diary*
Egmont, John Percival. *Manuscripts of the Earl of Egmont. Diary of Viscount Percival afterwards first Earl of Egmont.* . . . 3 vols. London: H.M. Stationery Office, 1920–1923.

Egmont, *Journal*
Egmont, John Percival, 1st Earl of. *Journal of the Earl of Egmont, First President of the Board of Trustees, from June 14, 1738, to May 25, 1744.* Vol. 5 of *Colonial Records of Georgia.* Atlanta GA: Franklin-Turner Co., 1908.

Ehrenhard, "Mapping for Archaeology"
Ehrenhard, John E. "Composite Mapping for Archaeology." In *Transactions of the First Conference of Scientific Research in the National Parks.* Houghton MI: Michigan Technological University, 1977.

Ellicott Journal
Journal of Andrew Ellicott, Late Commissioner on Behalf of the United States During Part of the Year 1796, the Years 1797, 1798, 1799, and Part of the Year 1800. Philadelphia: Printed by Budd & Bartram for Thomas Dobson, 1803.

Entry of Claims
Entry and Claims for Georgia Landholders, 1733–1755. Compiled by Pat Bryant. Atlanta: State Printing Office, 1975.

Ettinger, *Oglethorpe*
Ettinger, Amos A. *James Edward Oglethorpe, Imperial Idealist.* Hamden CT: Archon Books, 1968.

Eves, "Valley White"
Eves, Jamie H. "The Valley White with Mist: A Cape Cod Colony in Maine." *Maine Historical Society Quarterly* 32 (1992): 74-107.

Expedition Against the Spaniards
An Account of What the Army Did, under the Command of Col. [James] Moore, in His Expedition . . . Against the Spaniards . . . in a Letter . . . Printed in the Boston News, May 1, 1704.

Falconer, *Dictionary*
Falconer, William. *An Universal Dictionary of the Marine.* . . . New edition. London, 1780. Reprint, New York: Augustus M. Kelley, 1970.

Fauber, "Comprehensive Report"
Fauber, J. Everette. "A Comprehensive Report and a Proposal for the Restoration of Captain Horton's House on Jekyll Island, Georgia, Addressed to the Honorable Members of the Jekyll Island State Park Authority." Lynchburg VA, 10 April 1967. Unpublished manuscript. Copy at the Jekyll Island (Georgia) Authority.

Fisher, "Mary Musgrove"
Fisher, Doris Behrman. "Mary Musgrove: Creek Englishwoman." Ph.D. diss., Emory University, 1990.

Fleetwood, *Tidecraft*
    Fleetwood, William C., Jr. *Tidecraft: The Boats of South Carolina, Georgia, and Northeastern Florida, 1550–1950.* Tybee Island GA: W. B. G. Marine Press, 1995.

Franklin Papers
    Papers of Benjamin Franklin . . . 1766. Edited by Leonard W. Labaree et al. New Haven: Yale University Press, 1969–1993. [30 vols. to date]

G-Ar
    Georgia Department of Archives and History, Atlanta.

Ga Gaz
    Georgia Gazette (Savannah).

Gallardo, "Charles Town"
    Gallardo, Jose Miguel, ed. "The Spaniards and the English Settlement in Charles Town." *SCHGM* 37 (1936): 131-41.

Gallay, *Planter Elite*
    Gallay, Alan. *The Formation of a Planter Elite: Jonathan Bryan and the Southern Colonial Frontier.* Athens: University of Georgia Press, 1989.

Gay, *Medical Profession*
    Gay, Evelyn Ward. *The Medical Profession in Georgia, 1733–1983.* Atlanta: Auxiliary to the Medical Association of Georgia, 1983.

Georgia Memorials
    Georgia Land Owners' Memorials, 1758–1776. Abstracted by Eve B. Weeks and Robert S. Lowery. Edited by Mary Bondurant Warren. Danielsville GA: Heritage Papers, 1988.

Gerber, *Indigo*
    Gerber, Frederick H. *Indigo and the Antiquity of Dyeing.* Ormond Beach FL: Gerber, 1977.

GHi
    Georgia Historical Society, Savannah.

GHQ
    Georgia Historical Quarterly.

Ginger, *Oliver Goldsmith*
    Ginger, John. *The Notable Man: The Life and Times of Oliver Goldsmith.* London: Hamilton, 1977.

Glen, *Colonial South Carolina*
    Glen, James. *A Description of South Carolina. . . .* London: Printed for R. and J. Dodsley, 1761. Reprinted in *Colonial South Carolina: Two Contemporary Descriptions.* Edited by Chapman J. Milling. Columbia: University of South Carolina Press, 1951.

Gordon Journal
    The Journal of Peter Gordon, 1732–1735. Edited by E. Merton Coulter. Athens: University of Georgia Press, 1963.

Gray, *Agriculture*
    Gray, Lewis Cecil. *History of Agriculture in the Southern United States To 1860.* 2 vols. Washington, 1933. Reprint. Clifton NJ: Augustus M. Kelley, 1973.

Grimm, *Deutsches Wörterbuch*
  Grimm, Jacob, and Wilhelm Grimm. *Deutsches Wörterbuch*. Leipzig: Verlag von S. Hirzel,
  1893.
GU-HR
  Hargrett Rare Book and Manuscript Library, University of Georgia Libraries, Athens.
Hamer, "Anglo-French Rivalry"
  Hamer, P. M. "Anglo-French Rivalry in the Cherokee Country, 1754–1757." *North Carolina
  Historical Review* 2 (1925): 303-322.
Hamer, "Fort Loudoun"
  Hamer, P. M. "Fort Loudoun in the Cherokee War." *North Carolina Historical Review* 2
  (1925): 442-58.
Hardeman, *Corn in Pioneer America*
  Hardeman, Nicholas P. *Shucks, Shocks, and Hominy Blocks: Corn as a Way of Life in Pioneer
  America*. Baton Rouge: Louisiana State University Press, 1981.
Harman, *Trade and Privateering*
  Harman, Joyce Elizabeth. *Trade and Privateering in Spanish Florida, 1732–1763*. St.
  Augustine FL: St. Augustine Historical Society, 1969.
Hartridge Coll.
  Hartridge, Walter C., Jr., Collection. Georgia Historical Society, Savannah.
Hemperley, *Georgia's Boundaries*
  Hemperley, Marion R. *Georgia's Boundaries: The Shaping of a State*. Athens: Carl Vinson
  Institute of Government, University of Georgia, 1993.
Hemperley, *Historic Indian Trails*
  Hemperley, Marion R. *Historic Indian Trails of Georgia*. Atlanta: Garden Club of Georgia,
  1989.
Hershkowitz, *Wills of Early Jews*
  Hershkowitz, Leo. *Wills of Early New York Jews (1704–1799)*. Studies in American Jewish
  History, no. 4. New York: American Jewish Historical Society, 1967.
Hewatt, *Colonies*
  Hewatt, Alexander. *An Historical Account of the Rise and Progress of the Colonies of South
  Carolina and Georgia*. 2 vols. London: A. Donaldson, 1779.
Heyward, *Seeds from Madagascar*
  Heyward, Duncan Clinch. *Seeds from Madagascar*. Chapel Hill: University of North Carolina
  Press, 1937.
Hilliard, "Tidewater Rice Plantation"
  Hilliard, Sam B. "The Tidewater Rice Plantation: An Ingenious Adaptation to Nature," in
  Geoscience and Man. Vol. 12. Coastal Resources. Edited by H. J. Walker. Baton Rouge:
  School of Geoscience, Louisiana State University, 1975.
Hirsch, *Huguenots*
  Hirsch, H. H. *Huguenots of Colonial South Carolina*. Durham NC, 1928. Reprint, Hamden
  CT: Archon Books, 1962.

Historical Statistics

Historical Statistics of the United States. Colonial Times To 1940. Part 2. Washington: Bureau of the Census, 1975.

Hudson, *Southeastern Indians*

Hudson, Charles M. *The Southeastern Indians*. Knoxville: University of Tennessee Press, 1976.

Indian Affairs

Documents relating to Indian Affairs, May 21, 1750–August 7, 1754. Edited by William L. McDowell, Jr. Columbia: South Carolina Archives Department, 1958.

Ivers, *British Drums*

Ivers, Larry E. *British Drums on the Southern Frontier. The Military Colonization of Georgia, 1733–1749*. Chapel Hill: University of North Carolina Press, 1974.

Ivers, "Scouting the Inland Passage"

Ivers, Larry E. "Scouting the Inland Passage, 1685–1737." *SCHM* 73 (1972): 117-29.

Jackson, "Carolina Connection"

Jackson, Harvey H. "The Carolina Connection: Jonathan Bryan, His Brothers, and the Founding of Georgia, 1733–1752." *GHQ* 68 (1984): 147-72.

Jameson, *Privateering and Piracy*

Jameson, John Franklin. *Privateering and Piracy in the Colonial Period: Illustrative Documents*. New York: Macmillan Company, 1923. Reprint, New York: A. M. Kelley, 1970.

Johnston, *Houstouns of Georgia*

Johnston, Edith Duncan. *The Houstouns of Georgia*. Athens: University of Georgia Press, 1950.

Jones, *Dead Towns*

Jones, Charles C., Jr. *The Dead Towns of Georgia*. Savannah, 1878. Reprint, Spartanburg SC: Reprint Co., 1974.

Jones, *Georgia Dutch*

Jones, George Fenwick. *The Georgia Dutch: From the Rhine and Danube to the Savannah, 1733–1783*. Athens: University of Georgia Press, 1992.

Jones, *History of Augusta*

Jones, Charles C., Jr., and Salem Dutcher. *Memorial History of Augusta, Georgia, From its Settlement in 1735 to the Close of the Eighteenth Century*. Syracuse NY, 1890. Reprint. Spartanburg SC: Reprint Co., 1966.

Jones, *History of Georgia*

Jones, Charles C., Jr. *The History of Georgia*. 2 vols. Boston: Houghton, Mifflin and Co., 1883. Reprint. Spartanburg SC: Reprint Co., 1969.

Juricek, *Georgia Treaties*

Juricek, John T., ed. *Georgia Treaties, 1733–1763. Early American Indian Documents: Treaties and Laws, 1607–1789*. Alden T. Vaughan, general editor. 8 vols. Washington DC: University Publication of America, 1979–1994.

Keeval, *Medicine and the Navy*
Keeval, John J. *Medicine and the Navy, 1200–1900.* 4 vols. Edinburgh: E. & S. Livingstone, 1957–1963.

Kimber, *Expedition*
Kimber, Edward A. *A Relation or Journal of a Late Expedition to the Gates of St. Augustine on Florida, Conducted by the Hon. General James Oglethorpe with a Detachment of his Regiment, etc. from Georgia.* London, 1744. Reprint. Gainesville: University Presses of Florida, 1976.

Kimber, *Observations*
Kimber, Edward A. *Itinerant Observations in America. Reprinted from The London Magazine, 1745–6.* Savannah, 1878. Reprinted in Jones, *Dead Towns.*

Larson, *Aboriginal Subsistence*
Larson, Lewis H., Jr. *Aboriginal Subsistence Technology on the Southeastern Coastal Plain during the late Prehistoric Period.* Ripley P. Bullen Monographs and History, no. 2. Gainesville: University of Florida Press, 1980.

Larson, "Guale Indians"
Larson, Lewis H., Jr. "Guale Indians and the Spanish Mission Effort." In *Tacachale: Essays on the Indians of Florida and Southeastern Georgia during the Historic Periods. . . ,* no. 1. Edited by Jerald Milanich and Samuel Proctor. Gainesville: University of Florida, 1978.

Larson, "Spanish on Sapelo"
Larson, Lewis H., Jr. "The Spanish on Sapelo." In *Sapelo Papers: Researches in the History and Prehistory of Sapelo Island, Georgia.* West Georgia College Studies in the Social Sciences, vol. 19. Edited by Daniel P. Juengst. Carrollton: West Georgia College, June 1980.

Laurens Papers
The Papers of Henry Laurens. Edited by Philip Hamer and George C. Rogers, Jr. 13 vols. Columbia: University of South Carolina Press, 1968–1972.

Logan, "Journal"
"William Logan's Journal of a Journey to Georgia, 1745." *The Pennsylvania Magazine of History and Biography* 36 (1912): 1-16, 162-86.

Lovell, *Golden Isles*
Lovell, Caroline Couper. *The Golden Isles of Georgia.* Boston: Little, Brown and Co., 1932.

Ludlum, *Hurricanes*
Ludlum, David M. *Early American Hurricanes, 1492–1870.* Boston: American Meteorological Society, 1963.

McCall, *History of Georgia*
McCall, Hugh. *The History of Georgia, Containing Brief Sketches of the Most Remarkable Events Up to the Present Day, 1784.* Savannah, 1811–1816. Reprint, Atlanta: Cherokee Publishing Co., 1969.

Manucy, "Tabby"
Manucy, Albert A. "Tapia or Tabby." *Journal of the Society of Architectural Historians* 11 (1952): 32-33.

Marcus, *American Jewry*
   Marcus, Jacob Rader. *American Jewry: Documents, Eighteenth Century; Primarily Hitherto Unpublished Manuscripts.* Cincinnati: Hebrew Union College Press, 1959.
Marcus, *Colonial American Jew*
   Marcus, Jacob R. *The Colonial American Jew, 1492–1776.* 3 vols. Detroit: Wayne State University Press, 1970.
Marquardt, *Rigs & Rigging*
   Marquardt, Karl Heinz. *Eighteenth-century Rigs and Rigging.* Cedarburg WI: Phoenix Publications, 1992.
Marshall, "British Military Engineers"
   Marshall, Douglas William. "The British Military Engineers 1741–1783: A Study of Organization, Social Origin, and Cartography." Ph.D. diss., University of Michigan, 1976.
Martyn, *Impartial Inquiry*
   Martyn, Benjamin. *An Impartial Inquiry into the State and Utility of the Province of Georgia.* London, 1741. Reprinted in *CGHS*, 1:153-201. Savannah: The Society, 1840.
Mayo, *St. Marys River*
   Mayo, Lawrence Shaw. *The St. Marys River as a Boundary.* Cambridge MA: Privately printed, 1914.
Meriwether, *Expansion of SC*
   Meriwether, Robert L. *Expansion of South Carolina, 1729–1765.* Kingsport TN: Southern Publishers, 1940. Reprint. Philadelphia: Porcupine Press, 1974.
Milanich, "Alachua Tradition"
   Milanich, Jerald T., et al. "Georgia Origins of the Alachua Tradition." *Bureau of Historic Sites and Properties. Bulletin No. 5.* Division of Archives, History, and Records Management. Tallahassee FL: Department of State, 1979.
Milligan-Johnston, *Province of South-Carolina*
   Milligan-Johnston, George. *A Short History of the Province of South-Carolina . . . Written in the Year 1763.* London: Printed for J. Hinton, 1770.
Milling, *Red Carolinians*
   Milling, Chapman J. *Red Carolinians.* 2d ed. Columbia: University of South Carolina Press, 1969.
Moore, "Voyage to Georgia"
   Moore, Francis. *A Voyage to Georgia, begun in the year 1735. . . .* London: Printed for J. Robinson, 1744. Reprinted in *CGHS* (1840), 1:79-152.
Newell, "SC Vessel Types"
   Newell, Mark. "South Carolina Vessel Types." In Museum Small Craft Association, *19th Annual Conference Proceedings.* Thibodaux LA: Center for Traditional Louisiana Boat Building, Nicholls State University, 1992.
OED
   Oxford English Dictionary, 2d ed.

"Oglethorpe's Discourse"
  "James Oglethorpe's Introductory Discourse to the State of the Colony of Georgia." Phillips Collection of Egmont Manuscripts, 14204:123-35. Hargrett Rare Book and Manuscript Library, University of Georgia Libraries, Athens.

Oglethorpe's Georgia
  General Oglethorpe's Georgia: Colonial Letters, 1733–1743. 2 vols. Edited by Mills Lane. Savannah: Beehive Press, 1975.

Otto, "Open-Range Cattle Herding"
  Otto, John S. "Open-Range Cattle-Herding in Southern Florida." *Florida Historical Quarterly* 65 (1987): 317-34.

Parkman, *Waterways*
  Parkman, Aubrey. *History of the Waterways of the Atlantic Coast of the United States.* National Waterways Study, U.S. Army Engineer Water Resources Support Center, Institute for Water Resources, pub. in series, Navigation History, NWS-83-10, January 1983.

Phillips, *Companion for the Orchard*
  Phillips, Henry. *The Companion for the Orchard.* London: H. Colburn and R. Bentley, 1831.

Phillips, *Labor in the Old South*
  Phillips, Ulrich Bonnell. *Life and Labor in the Old South.* Boston: Little, Brown and Company, 1957.

Pool, *Portraits in Stone*
  Pool, David De Sola. *Portraits Etched in Stone: Early Jewish Settlers, 1682–1831.* New York: Columbia University Press, 1952.

"Pringle Journal"
  "Journal of Robert Pringle, 1746–1747." *SCHGM* 26 (1925): 21-30; 93-112.

Privy Council
  Acts of the Privy Council of England. Colonial Series. A.D. 1613–1783. Edited by James Munro. 6 vols. London: H.M. Stationery Office, 1908–1912.

PRO
  Public Record Office, Kew, Richmond, Surrey UK.

"Proceedings"
  "Proceedings of the President and Assistants in Council of Georgia, 1749–1751." Edited by Lilla M. Hawes. *GHQ* 35, Part 1 (1951): 323-50; 36, Part 2 (1952): 46-70.

Ramsey, "Fort William"
  Ramsey, William. "The Final Contest for 'Debatable Land': Fort William and the Frontier Defenses of Colonial Georgia." *GHQ* 77 (1993): 497-524.

Redding, *Jonathan Bryan*
  Redding, Mrs. J. H. *The Life and Times of Jonathan Bryan, 1708–1788.* Savannah: Morning News Print, 1901.

Reitz, "Colonial Experience"
  Reitz, Elizabeth J. "The Spanish Colonial Experience and Domestic Animals." *Historical Archaeology* 26 (1992): 84-91.

Revolutionary Records

    Revolutionary Records of the State of Georgia. Compiled by Allen Daniel Candler. 3 vols. Atlanta GA, 1908. Reprint. New York: AMS Press, 1972.

Romans, "Map"

    Romans, Bernard A. "General Map of the Southern British Colonies in America." In *American Military Pocket Atlas* (1776).

Romans, *Natural History*

    Romans, Bernard A. *Concise Natural History of East and West Florida.* New York: Printed for the author, 1775. Reprint, Gainesville: University of Florida Press, 1962.

Root, *Food*

    Root, Waverly. *Food, An Authoritative and Visual History and Dictionary of the Foods of the World.* New York: Simon and Schuster, 1980.

Rosenbloom, *Early American Jews*

    Rosenbloom, Joseph R. *A Biographical Dictionary of Early American Jews: Colonial Times through 1800.* Lexington: University of Kentucky Press, 1960.

Rostlund, "Historic Bison"

    Rostlund, Erhard. "The Geographic Range of the Historic Bison in the Southeast." *Annals of the Association of American Geographers* 50 (1960): 395-407.

Runnette, "Stoney Creek Cemetery"

    Runnette, Mabel. "Inscriptions in Stoney Creek Cemetery." *SCHGM* 37 (1936): 100-110.

Ruple, "Horton House"

    Ruple, Steven D. "Archaeology at Horton House." Master's thesis, University of Florida, 1976. Copy at the Jekyll Island (Georgia) Authority.

Salley, *Register of St. Philip's Parish*

    Salley, A. S., Jr. *Register of St. Philip's Parish, Charles Town, South Carolina, 1720–1758.* Columbia: University of South Carolina Press, 1971.

Savannah River Plantations

    Savannah River Plantations. Edited by Mary Granger. Savannah: Georgia Historical Society, 1947. Reprint. Spartanburg SC: Reprint Co., 1972.

SC Gaz

    South Carolina Gazette and Public Advertiser (Charleston).

SC Wills, 1670–1740

    Abstracts of the Wills of the State of South Carolina, 1670–1740. Compiled and edited by Caroline T. Moore. Columbia SC: The compiler, 1960.

SC Wills, 1740–1760

    Abstracts of the Wills of the State of South Carolina, 1740–1760. Compiled and edited by Caroline T. Moore. Columbia SC: The compiler, 1964.

SCHGM

    South Carolina Historical and Genealogical Magazine.

SCHM

    South Carolina Historical Magazine.

Schoepf, *Travels*
Schoepf, Johann David. *Travels in the Confederation, 1783–1784.* Translated and edited by Alfred J. Morrison. 2 vols. Philadelphia: W. J. Campbell, 1911. Reprint. New York: Burt Franklin, 1968.

Serrano y Sanz, "Relación del Yndio."
Serrano y Sanz, Manuel, editor. "Relación del Yndio." *Documentos Históricos de la Florida y la Luisiana, Siglos XVI al XVIII.* Madrid: Libreria General de Victoriana Suarez, 1912.

Sheftall, *Sunbury*
Sheftall, John McKay. *Sunbury on the Medway: A Selective History of the Town, Inhabitants, and Fortifications.* Atlanta: State of Georgia, Department of Natural Resources, Historic Preservation Section, 1977.

Smith, *Fort San Carlos*
Smith, Hale G., and Ripley P. Bullen. *Fort San Carlos.* Notes in Anthropology, vol. 14. Tallahassee: Florida State University, 1971.

Spalding, "James Oglethorpe"
Spalding, Thomas. "Sketch of the Life of General James Oglethorpe." *CGHS*, 1:239-95. Savannah: The Society, 1840.

Spalding, "Tabby"
Spalding, Thomas, "On the mode of Constructing Tabby buildings, and the propriety of improving our plantations in a permanent manner." *Southern Agriculturist* 3 (1830): 617-24.

Spanish Official Account
The Spanish Official Account of the Attack on the Colony of Georgia, in America, and of its Defeat on St. Simons Island by General James Oglethorpe. Savannah: Georgia Historical Society, 1913.

Stacy, *Midway*
Stacy, James. *History and Published Records of the Midway Congregational Church, Liberty County, Georgia.* Spartanburg SC: Reprint Co., 1979. Reprint of *History of Midway Congregational Church . . .* published in 1903 and of *The Published Records of Midway Church*, vol. 1, published in 1894; and of the addenda by E. W. Quarterman published with the revised history in 1951.

Steel's Elements of Mastmaking
Steel's Elements of Mastmaking, Sailmaking and Rigging (From the 1794 Edition). London: W. & G. Foyle, 1932.

Stephens, *Journal 1741–1743*
The Journal of William Stephens, 1741–1743. Edited by E. Merton Coulter. Athens: University of Georgia Press, 1958.

Stephens, *Journal 1743–1745*
The Journal of William Stephens, 1743–1745. Edited by E. Merton Coulter. Athens: University of Georgia Press, 1959.

Stern, *American Jewish Families*
   Stern, Malcolm H., compiler. *First American Jewish Families.* Cincinnati OH: American Jewish Archives, 1978.
Stern, "Sheftall Diaries"
   Stern, Malcolm H. "The Sheftall Diaries: Vital Records of Savannah Jewry (1733–1808)." *American Jewish Historical Quarterly* 54 (1965): 243-77.
Stevens, *History of Georgia*
   Stevens, William Bacon. *A History of Georgia.* 2 vols. New-York: D. Appleton and Co., 1847–1859.
Sullivan, *McIntosh County*
   Sullivan, Buddy. *Early Days on the Georgia Tidewater: The Story of McIntosh County & Sapelo.* Darien GA: McIntosh County Board of Commissioners, 1990.
Tailfer, *Narrative*
   Tailfer, Patrick, et al. *A True and Historical Narrative of the Colony of Georgia, in America, From the First Settlement Thereof until this Present Period. . . .* Charleston, 1741. Other editions.
Taylor, *Georgia Plan*
   Taylor, Paul S. *Georgia Plan: 1732–1752.* Berkeley: Institute of Business and Economic Research, Graduate School of Business Administration, University of California, 1972.
Temple, *Georgia Journeys*
   Temple, Sarah B. Gover, and Kenneth Coleman. *Georgia Journeys, Being an Account of the Lives of Georgia's Original Settlers and Many Other Early Settlers from the Founding of the Colony in 1732 until the Institution of Royal Government in 1754.* Athens: University of Georgia Press, 1961.
Thomas, "Saints and Soldiers"
   Thomas, David Hurst. "Saints and Soldiers at Santa Catalina: Hispanic Designs for Colonial America." In *The Recovery of Meaning: Historical Archaeology in the Eastern United States.* Edited by Mark P. Leone and Parker B. Potter, Jr. Washington DC: Smithsonian Institution Press, 1988.
Thomas, "Spanish Mission Experience"
   Thomas, David Hurst. "The Spanish Mission Experience in La Florida," in *Columbus and the Land of Ayllón. The Exploration and Settlement of the Southeast.* Edited by Jeannine Cook. Darien GA: Lower Altamaha Historical Society-Ayllón, 1992.
Thomas, *St. Catherine*
   Thomas, David Hurst. *St. Catherine: An Island in Time.* Atlanta: Georgia Humanities Council, 1988.
Tinkler, *Atlantic Intracoastal Waterway*
   Tinkler, William P. *The U.S. Army Corps of Engineers, Atlantic Intracoastal Waterway Project in Georgia: A Study of Its History, Maintenance, and Present Use.* Rev. ed. Brunswick GA: Georgia Department of Natural Resources, 1976.

Todd, *Prince William's Parish*
   Todd, John R., and Francis Hutson. *Prince William's Parish and Plantations*. Richmond: Garnett and Massie, 1935.
Treasury Books and Papers
   Calendar of Treasury Books and Papers, 1729–1745. 5 vols. London: H.M. Stationery Office, 1903.
Vignoles, *Observations*
   Vignoles, Charles. *Observations upon the Floridas*. New York: E. Bliss, 1823.
Von Reck's Voyage
   Von Reck's Voyage: Drawings and Journal of Philip George Fredrich von Reck, ed. Kristian Hvidt. Savannah: Beehive Press, 1980.
"Weather in Georgia"
   "An Account of the Heat of the Weather in Georgia: In a Letter from his Excellency Henry Ellis, Esq., Governor of Georgia. . . . " *London Magazine* (July 1759): 371-72.
Weber, *Spanish Frontier*
   Weber, David J. *The Spanish Frontier in North America*. New Haven: Yale University Press, 1992.
White, *Statistics*
   White, George. *Statistics of the State of Georgia*. . . . Savannah: W. Thorne Williams, 1849. Reprint. Spartanburg SC: Reprint Co., 1972.
Williams, "British-American Officers"
   Williams, W. R., comp. "British-American Officers, 1720 to 1763." *SCHGM* 33 (1932): 183-96, 259-96.
Wilson, *Drugs and Pharmacy*
   Wilson, Robert C. *Drugs and Pharmacy in the Life of Georgia, 1733–1958*. Athens: University of Georgia Press, 1959.
Wilson, *Food & Drink*
   Wilson, C. Anne. *Food & Drink in Britain*. London: Constable & Co., 1973.
Wilson, *Liberty County*
   Wilson, Carolyn Price. *Annals of Georgia . . . Liberty County Records*. . . . New York, 1928. Reprint, Vidalia GA: Georgia Genealogical Reprints, 1969.
Wilson, "Missing Salzburger Diaries"
   Wilson, Renata. "Public Works and Piety in Ebenezer: The Missing Salzburger Diaries of 1744–1745." *GHQ* 77 (1993): 336-66.
Winberry, "Carolina Indigo"
   Winberry, John T. "Reputation of Carolina Indigo." *SCHM* 80 (1979): 242-50.
Wood, *Live Oaking*
   Wood, Virginia Steele. *Live Oaking: Southern Timber for Tall Ships*. Boston: Northeastern University Press, 1981. Reprint. Annapolis MD: Naval Institute Press, 1995.

Worth, *Georgia Coast*

    Worth, John E. *The Struggle for the Georgia Coast: An Eighteenth-Century Spanish Retrospective on Guale and Mocama.* Anthropological Papers of the American Museum of Natural History, no. 75, 1995; distributed by the University of Georgia Press, 1995.

Wright, *Georgia-Florida Frontier*

    Wright, Albert Hazen. *Our Georgia-Florida Frontier.* Ithaca NY: A. H. Wright, 1945.

Wright, *Map*

    A Map of Georgia and Florida taken from the latest and most accurate surveys . . . by Thos. Wright. Map G 3870 (1763), GU-HR. Photostatic copy from PRO also in the Georgraphy and Map Division, DLC.

Notes

1. The term "Indian Land" referred to old Indian reserves in South Carolina from which St. Helena and Prince William Parishes later derived. In 1686 a strip of territory between the Edisto and Savannah Rivers was inhabited by the Yamassee alone, except for a few white traders. After 1702, when the Yamassee fled to Florida, the term "Indian Land" covered a very large area north of the Savannah River. In the 1720s the Southern Rangers, patrolling the thickets and swamps of the Edisto, Ashepoo, and Combahee Rivers, were constantly on the alert for Yamassee war parties who raided the frontier from their sanctuary in Spanish Florida. Even in 1727 the Indian Land was so deserted that the Yamassee could strike almost at will.

When Gen. James Oglethorpe made his first treaty with the Creek Nation on behalf of the Crown in 1733, it defined the area reserved by the Indians for their own use, stating that it would be created between Pallachucola Creek and Pipemakers Bluff. This treaty was renewed and extended on 21 August 1739 when Oglethorpe made another one with the Creek Nations on behalf of the Trustees. Not only was the land cession of 1733 reaffirmed and more fully described, but the Creeks reserved for themselves the "Lands from Pipe Makers Bluff to Savannah and the Islands of St. Catherine, Useba and Sappala." In 1757, at a congress held at Savannah, a treaty between the English and Creeks gave to Georgia the three great Sea Islands and a small tract—also known as the "Indian Land"—near Savannah. Subsequently, the phrase tended to fade out in Georgia.

On the South Carolina side of the Savannah River, however, the term "Indian Land" continued in use somewhat longer and referred to a long strip, contiguous to the Savannah River, that included the settlements of Purrysburgh, Yamassee, and Pocotaligo, comprising St. Helena Parish. From the upper part of St. Helenas a new parish called Prince Williams was carved out in 1745, and included the Stoney Creek Independent Presbyterian Church built near Pocotaligo. When the writer of this journal referred to his plantations in Prince William Parish, he was simply using the old terminology "Indian Land." Even in the late eighteenth century some old-timers were still referring to it this way. The 1785 obituary of Col. William Harden, for example, stated that he "died in Prince Williams Parish, Indian Land." It is well to note that in the old Southeast there were several areas called "the Indian Land." Milling, *Red Carolinians*, 104; Crane, *Southern Frontier*, 164, 189, 215; Todd, *Prince William's Parish*, passim; Runnette, "Stoney Creek Cemetery," 37: 100 n. 1; *Colonial Records of SC*, 12:386, 14:73; *SC Gaz*, 3 December 1785. John T. Juricek to Mary R. Bullard, personal communication, 13 February 1993.

2. Jonathan Bryan was born 12 September 1708 at Port Royal, South Carolina, the youngest child of planter and Indian trader Joseph Bryan and his wife Janet Cochran, both English emigrants who arrived in Carolina by 1697. As a youth assisting his father Jonathan formed close ties with many Creeks and developed better ways of dealing with the Indians

than did his father, who was accused of committing murderous depredations against them. Jonathan learned how to carve piraguas from cypress and cedar logs, Indian style, and was a superb boatman almost from childhood.

With the arrival of James Oglethorpe and the first Georgia settlers, Jonathan and his brothers took an active role in the new colony by donating free labor, supplying goods to the settlers at reasonable prices, provisioning the military, and helping sponsor the orphanage at Bethesda. Jonathan, in fact, became one of General Oglethorpe's closest associates and was present during important negotiation with the Indians. He also became an ardent follower of dissenter George Whitefield (1714–1770) when the noted evangelist was sent to Frederica from England by the Trustees in 1737. Abandoning the Church of England in 1743, Jonathan, his brother Hugh, and many of their neighbors formed an Independent Presbyterian congregation which accepted slaves as members.

On 13 October 1737 Bryan married Mary Williamson (ca. 1721–1781), aged sixteen, also of South Carolina. The couple had thirteen children, seven of whom died in childhood or as young adults. His heavy white taffeta wedding vest at Telfair Academy in Savannah, which dwarfs other garments on exhibit, helps corroborate the statement that Bryan was "a tall and large man, of wonderful strength and hardihood, and of imposing appearance" (White, *Statistics*, 126).

He also possessed the attributes of intelligence, leadership, adaptability, religious tolerance, a hospitable nature, and social adeptness. As a member of a family of Port Royal traders in the early 1700s, though, he had no social standing among the elite of Charleston society. Jonathan, and his brother Hugh (an unusually competent surveyor), with their great ability made a conscious effort to develop Port Royal as an important trading center. It is said that they "devoted extraordinary energy to the pursuit of both profit and improving the lot of others" (Gallay, *Planter Elite*, 23). After his move to Georgia, Jonathan worked diligently to develop the port of Savannah as well as new ports on the rivers Altamaha and Apalachicola. There, his abilities recognized, he was asked to serve on the royal governor's council, he was a justice of the general court, he was appointed treasurer by the governor, and he held other public offices.

During the American Revolution the patriotic activities of Bryan and his son James resulted in their capture during 1778, followed by a miserable confinement in British prison hulks off Long Island, New York. Despite his age, Bryan allegedly kept his health by obtaining permission to swim around the hulk once each day. The two men were finally exchanged in 1781, but too late to reach home before the death of Bryan's wife, Mary. Jonathan was subsequently appointed to the state's executive council and lived out his days at Brampton plantation on the Savannah River. He died 12 March 1788 and was buried near family members in the small cemetery at Brampton on property now controlled by the National Gypsum Company. Surrounded by a brick wall, the graves are some 200 feet from the river Bryan knew so well. Five years after his death, Bryan County, Georgia, was named in his honor. Photocopies of family record pages of Jonathan Bryan's family Bible (London:

Printed by John Baskett, 1739) and notes from the Bible are in the Hartridge Coll.; notes on the Bryan family cemetery at Brampton made during a visit by Sarah N. Pinckney, Savannah, Georgia, discussed in a telephone conversation with Virginia S. Wood, 17 January 1994; *Savannah Morning News Magazine*, 15 September 1963. For details of Bryan's life see Gallay, *Planter Elite*; Jackson, "Carolina Connection"; Redding, *Jonathan Bryan*. See also *Gordon Journal*, 43; White, *Statistics*, 126; Johnston, *Houstouns of Georgia*, 229.

3. Athens: University of Georgia Press, 1989.

4. *The History of Georgia*, 2 vols. (New York: D. Appleton Co., 1847–1859), 1:405.

5. Jones, *Dead Towns*, 127; Lovell, *Golden Isles*, 64; Bullard, "Cumberland Island's Dungeness," 76 n. 19.

6. Isaac Levy (1706–1777), merchant and commercial agent, a son of Moses and Rebecca (Asher) Levy, was probably born in London, but he resided in New York and Philadelphia as well as Boston. In 1754 Thomas Bosomworth and his wife Mary Musgrove visited London to obtain approval of their claim to the Georgia islands of St. Catherines, Ossabaw, and Sapelo, the gift of a Creek chief. In need of funds to remain solvent, they accepted £200 sterling from Levy in exchange for a moiety (a half-interest) in all three islands and his offer to petition the king on their behalf. If successful he was to pay the Bosomworths an additional £100; if not, they were to repay the money that Levy advanced. Unfortunately, neither the Bosomworths nor Levy achieved success in obtaining title from Commissioners of the Board of Trade or the Privy Council, both asserting that such lands were for tribal use and could not be disposed of by an individual in the tribe. Eventually, the British gave St. Catherines plus £1,200 sterling to Mary Musgrove. Levy and his lawyer spent several frustrating years submitting memorials and affidavits to support Levy's claim, but to no avail.

Finally, in lieu of his moiety in the Georgia islands, Levy petitioned for "some ceded lands in the West Indies or the coal mine in the Island of Cape Briton [Cape Breton, Nova Scotia]," for a term of years, but this, too, was denied him by the Board of Trade. In 1769 an Isaac Levy and a dozen other men obtained a grant of some 13,000 acres located on the west bank of the Hudson River. If this is the same as the Isaac Levy mentioned above, his alliance with the influential Franks and De Lancey families of New York and London may be the reason they were successful. As such he "was one of the few Jews in America who could muster influence with the provincial authorities, if not with the Lords of Trade" (Marcus, *Colonial American Jew*, 3:765). Isaac Levy died in Philadelphia in March 1777.

Any evidence that he had direct contact with Georgia prior to 1754 remains elusive, although seeking it was not the editors' primary focus. During the 1740s the Levy-Franks combine moved to Philadelphia, and between 1744 and 1751 they owned several vessels that were no doubt used in their "extensive operations as American agents for the London consortium of army suppliers," from Quebec to ports in the South (Marcus, *Colonial American Jew,* 3:617, 627). Unfortunately, few of their papers have survived. An unidentified Isaac Levy arrived in Savannah from London in August 1736 (Stern, "Sheftall Diaries," 248). The editors suggest that Samson Levy (1722–1781), Isaac's half-brother, was the same as merchant Sampson Levi to whom the Trustees made a partial payment of £600 in August 1739 "for stores supply'd in Georgia" (Egmont, *Journal,* 215). In October 1741 William Stephens made two tantalizing entries in his journals, but in neither instance included a first name: "Mr *Levi*" who went to Frederica on 13 October, returned to Savannah on 26 October saying that he and "the General" [Oglethorpe] agreed on the price of 150 casks of flour, but without a written order. Three days later "Mr Levi" returned to Charles Town. (*CRG,* 4, Supplement, 273; Stephens, *Journal 1741–1743,* 1).

The half-brothers were evidently very close. In his will Isaac Levy directed that should his children die before reaching the age of twenty-one, the estate was to be divided between his brother Samson and his sister Rachell; Isaac Levy's son Asher, along with Samson and his son Moses, were named executors.

It is worthwhile noting that there were several individuals named Isaac Levy in colonial America; Levi Sheftall mentioned one who arrived in Savannah from London on 31 August 1736, but his identity is unknown to the editors. Bosomworth Controversy Papers, Peter Force Transcripts, Manuscript Division, DLC; Fisher, "Mary Musgrove"; *SC Gaz,* 20 October 1759; Marcus, *Colonial American Jew,* 3:763-65; Hershkowitz, *Wills of Early Jews,* 36-40, 158-60; *Calendar of State Papers,* 215; *Privy Council,* 4:312-16, 5:114-15, 600; *Board of Trade, 1750–1753,* 328, 256, *1754–1758,* 392, *1759–1763,* 80, 156-57, *1759–1763,* 8057, *1764–1767,* 53, 93, 94, 100-101, 406, *1768–1775,* 6, 7, 12, 13, 41, 44; *CRG,* 5:44, 215; 8:171; 28, Pt. 1: 22-23, 91-98, 133, 219-30; 28, Pt. 2: 6, 43-47, 213-15, 239-43, 247-51; Marcus, *American Jewry,* 218-22; Stephens, *Journal 1741–1743,* 1; Pool, *Portraits in Stone,* 225-26; Stern, *American Jewish Families,* 154; Stern, "Sheftall Diaries," 248; Rosenbloom, *Early American Jews,* 92; Hemperley, *Georgia's Boundaries,* 50-51.

7. Stevens, *History of Georgia,* 1:227.

8. Coulter, *Joseph Vallence Bevan,* 74.

9. On the other hand, several autographed letters of Jonathan Bryan are listed. *Catalogue of I. K. Tefft,* 23. See also *DGB,* 2:932-33, 964-65.

10. In 1937 the journal was not cited as a reference in Marmaduke Floyd, "Certain Tabby Ruins on the Georgia Coast," *Disputed Ruins*, 3-passim.

11. "Barnwell's Journal," 193.

12. L. H. Butterfield, in his introduction to *The Adams Papers*, 4 vols. (Cambridge: Harvard University Press, 1961), 1: lxvi n. 9; Cline, *Women's Diaries*, vii-viii.

13. Thomas L. Gravell to Virginia S. Wood, 19 August 1993; Virginia S. Wood, telephone interview with Thomas L. Gravell, Wilmington, Delaware, 20 August 1993.

14. *CRG*, 6:333-34, 369.

15. *CRG*, 1:530-32; 2:500, 514, 522.

16. *Council Journal 1753–1760*, v, vi ff; Stevens, *History of Georgia*, 1:280-82; Jones, *History of Georgia*, 1:312-13, 428; Taylor, *Georgia Plan*, 291-92; *Savannah River Plantations*, introduction, n.p. [xx].

17. The birth of Bryan's ninth child, James, on 22 September 1752 may have delayed their move until December. Notations "Taken from the Bible of Jonathan Bryan by his Great-grand Daughter, Georgia H. Screvin," Hartridge Coll.

18. One gleans some measure of Bryan's ability to get along with disparate groups of people if the scouts he commanded in 1733 had the same propensities as those who served under Colonel John Barnwell a decade earlier: "These Scoutmen are a wild Idle people & Continually Sotting if they can gett any Rum for Trust or money. Yet they are greatly usefull for Such Expeditions as these if well & Tenderly managed, ffor as their Chiefest Imploy is to hunt the fforest or ffish, So there is Scarce One of Them but understands the Hoe, the Axe, the Saw, as well as their Gun and Oar" ("Barnwell's Journal," 193).

19. Moore, "Voyage to Georgia," 130.

20. Deposition of Jonathan Bryan "of St. Helens in the County of Berkley [*sic*] in the Province of Carolina" signed 30 March 1736 before Francis Moore, Recorder of the Town of Frederica, colony of Georgia, and sworn to on the same date at Frederica by Francis Moore. *CRG*, 35:36, unpublished transcript MS, G-Ar.

21. Ivers, *British Drums*, 105-32.

22. Jonathan Bryan to George Whitefield, 1 July 1753. George Whitefield Papers, Manuscript Division, DLC. Gallay interpreted the date as 4 July 1753. See Gallay, *Planter Elite*, 228 n. 59.

23. Chesnutt, *South Carolina's Expansion*, 147. See appendix 3, "Jonathan Bryan's Petitions for Land in Georgia," and appendix 4, "Conveyances of Land and other Property to and from Jonathan Bryan," in Gallay, *Planter Elite*, 171-83; *Georgia Memorials*, see index.

24. This total figure of whites and slaves, reported 11 April 1753 to the Board of Trade, excluded military personnel. Population figures provided by the U.S. government give Georgia's estimated population for 1750 as 5,200; for 1760 as 9,578. Jones, *History of Georgia*, 1:459-60; *Historical Statistics*, 1168.

25. *CRG*, 27:200, 201, 265; 28, Pt. 2: 24-25; Fisher, "Mary Musgrove," 416. For a discussion of Georgia's early boundaries, see Hemperley, *Georgia's Boundaries*, 14-18, 46-50.

26. Tabby is a mixture of sand, water, lime burned from abundant oyster shells, and broken pieces of shells, all formed in wooden molds. When thoroughly hardened tabby could be cut into building blocks as one would cut stone. See Spalding, "Tabby" 24; Manucy, "Tabby"; *Disputed Ruins*, 72-76.

27. Abbot, *Royal Governors*. These were German Salzburgers who emigrated to Georgia to avoid religious persecution. See Jones, *Georgia Dutch*.

28. Jones, *History of Augusta*, 35-37; Cashin, *Colonial Augusta*, 63-68.

29. *CRG*, 26:355; *Abercromby Letter Book*, 15-16 n. 8; Jones, *History of Georgia*, 1:426-27; McCall, *History of Georgia*, 1:211. It is worthwhile noting that in 1753 it would be another decade before the colony had her own newspaper, the *Georgia Gazette*, published in Savannah.

30. Kimber, *Observations*, 12-13.

31. *CRG*, 35:557.

32. Gov. Henry Ellis was unambiguous in his reaction to summertime in the colony: "such is the debilitating quality of our violent heats at this season, that an expressible languor [*sic*] enervates every faculty, and renders even the thought of exercising them

painful" ("Weather in Georgia"). In December 1758 the Privy Council granted Ellis the same privilege granted to governors in the West Indies—to visit a northern colony "to recover his health . . . much impaired by the extraordinary heat of the last summer" (*Privy Council*, 4:397).

33. Variant spellings include piragua, periagua, periauger, pereauger, and so on. Each oarsman, stationed at a single oar, required about forty inches of space to be effective. With ten crew members, four passengers, and cargo stowage, Bryan's boat would probably have been at least forty feet in length. Lawrence E. Babits, Program in Maritime History and Underwater Research, Dept. of History, East Carolina University, to Virginia S. Wood, 23 December 1993; Fleetwood, *Tidecraft*, 31-43.

34. Francis Moore described these vessels that transported settlers from Port Royal and Savannah to Frederica in 1734 as having a capacity of twenty to thirty-five tons. *CGHS*, 1:112-13.

35. Babits to Wood, 23 December 1993; Fleetwood, *Tidecraft*, 31-38; Alford, "Boat Building," 20-25; Newell, "SC Vessel Types," 26-41.

36. John Reynolds, first royal governor of Georgia, called on De Brahm to survey the colony's fortifications and make recommendations. In 1756 Reynolds submitted De Brahm's economical plan specifying the types of forts, the ordinance, and the number of men needed, but the Board of Trade was unmoved, and "the defenses of Georgia were suffered to remain in a deplorable condition." Jones, *History of Georgia*, 1: 505-10.

37. Indeed, it was thought "the land was 'improved' by transforming forests into fields, trees into lumber, and fish into food" (Eves, "Valley White," 76). Extolling nature's rich and apparent inexhaustible bounty, an untitled poem found in 1776 was printed a decade later in the Falmouth, Maine, *Gazette* (14 January 1786), concluding:

> These precious gifts, with numbers more
> Which might be added to the score,
> Were made to serve the use of man,
> When first the world and time began.

This echoed the Biblical admonition in Genesis (1:28) to "Be fruitful, and multiply, and replenish the earth, and subdue it, and have domination over . . . every living thing that moveth upon the earth"—a message chilling to present-day environmentalists and conservationists. Eves, "Valley White"; Blaitie, *Land Degradation*.

38. *CRG,* 5:41, 165, 454, 503, 540; Egmont, *Journal,* 35-36, 38, 59, 72-73, passim.

39. It was a style made famous by John Dryden (1631–1700) and Alexander Pope (1688–1744). Examples of these are found in a myriad of British literary magazines of the period, and publishers often lifted poems without permission and printed them in *Gentleman's Magazine* and the *London Magazine;* excerpts occasionally appeared in the early *South-Carolina Gazette.* Most young men who had a tutor—even briefly—could have burst into heroic verse, although not necessarily very good verse. It was fairly easy to write, and a stilted vocabulary was commonplace. A tin ear for meter was no handicap. Oliver Goldsmith (1728–1774), a contemporary of Bryan, demonstrated the ease with which one could compose such verse. The literary critic Ginger, who included the following gem, wrote that Goldmith's family passed down the story that he tossed off this couplet as a young boy after attending his father's church one Sunday:

> A pious rat for want of stairs
> Came down the rope to say his prayers.

Ginger, *Oliver Goldsmith,* 38.

40. Corkran, *Creek Frontier,* 114; Reitz, "Colonial Experience"; Weber, *Spanish Frontier,* 110-11; Ivers, *British Drums,* 182.

41. Otto, "Open-Range Cattle-Herding," 331 n. 74; Corkran, *Creek Frontier,* 114.

42. Root, *Food,* 236.

43. *CRG,* 3:407.

44. Gray, *Agriculture,* 161, 171; Bonner, *Georgia Agriculture,* 21-22; Root, *Food,* 235-38; Tailfer, *Narrative,* 29, 101-103; *CRG,* 2:337; Hardeman, *Corn in Pioneer America.* Benjamin Franklin considered roasted ears of corn "a delicacy beyond expression" and thought that "a *johny* or *hoecake,* hot from the fire, is better than a Yorkshire muffin." *Franklin Papers,* 13:7.

45. Tailfer, *Narrative,* 102-103.

46. *CRG,* 1:278, 287; 2:177; 3:62; Schoepf, *Travels,* 1:182; Hewatt, *Colonies,* 2:182.

47. Phillips, *Labor in the Old South,* 50; Hewatt, *Colonies,* 2:159; 1:85, 159.

48. *CRG*, 1:278, 287; 2:177; 3:62, 422-26, 500, 531-32.

49. Hilliard, "Tidewater Rice Plantation," 57. See also De Brahm, *Report*, 162; Coon, "Market Agriculture," 164-70, passim.

50. William De Brahm calculated that the expense of clearing and planting 130 acres in rice with forty slaves amounted to £2,476.16.0. De Brahm, *Report*, 162-63. See also *Argyle Island*, x-xiii; Hilliard, "Tidewater Rice Plantation," 58-61. Remnants of old rice fields are still visible in South Carolina and Georgia. One of these is in the Altamaha River delta along U.S. 17 between Darien and Brunswick, Georgia.

51. Heyward, *Seeds from Madagascar*, 1937, 14; Gray, *Agriculture*, 1:280.

52. *Savannah River Plantations*, introduction, n.p., reprinted from *GHQ* 22 (1938): 314.

53. Stephens, *Journal 1743–1745*, 106; *CRG*, 4:664; Taylor, *Georgia Plan*, 117.

54. Harman, *Trade and Privateering*, 14-17, 21-24.

55. "Pringle Journal," 96, 102; Phillips, *Companion for the Orchard*, 216-19; Wilson, *Food & Drink*, 353, 357, 401; Keeval, *Medicine and the Navy*, 3:112-13, 299, 321-22.

56. Glen, *Colonial South Carolina*, 29.

57. *CRG*, 4:664, 7:101; Downing, *Fruit Trees of America*, 542; Glen, *Colonial South Carolina*, 37.

58. Buchanan, *Weaver's Garden*, 102.

59. Apparently, Carolina indigo never attained the high quality of dye produced by the French and Spanish in the West Indies and later in India. Winberry, "Carolina Indigo"; *CRG*, 1:362, 25:55; Gerber, *Indigo*, 25; Buchanan, *Weaver's Garden*, 102-109.

60. Stephens, *Journal, 1743–1745*, 185; De Brahm, *Report*, 72, 214; Hirsch, *Huguenots*, 214-17; Act for encouraging the making of Indico [*sic*] in the British Plantations in America, 22 Geo. 3, c. 30; *Abercromby Letter Book*, 137; Gray, *Agriculture*, 291-93; Bonner, *Georgia Agriculture*, 18-20; *Board of Trade*, 212.

61. Patrick Graham (?–1755), surgeon and apothecary of Crieff, Scotland, arrived in Georgia at his own expense. The Trustees initially granted him a lot in Savannah; he rented two others, and in 1736 they granted him a 100-acre tract. By 1739 he relinquished his medical practice and became "so industrious a Planter that he maintain'd himself" (*CRG*, 5:557). In 1743 Graham became an Assistant on Georgia's Board of President and Assistants and soon afterward served as President. It was in this capacity that he signed the permit for Jonathan Bryan and his companions to have the use of a scout boat and armed crew for their journey from St. Simons to Florida in August 1753. (The Assistants were James Habersham, Noble Jones, Pickering Robinson, and Francis Harris.) Graham was also one of His Majesty's agents to distribute presents to the Indians, and after Georgia became a Royal Province in 1754, he served on the Governor's Council.

On 6 March 1739/1740 Graham married Anne Cuthbert, and the circumstances of their courtship were set down by William Stephens: "Mr. Patrick Graham, Surgeon, who has made considerable Improvement in Building on his Lot in this Town, as well as been a constant Planter for two or three Years past, having Mrs. Cuthbert (Sister to the late Capt. [John] Cuthbert, deceased) for his Patient dangerously ill in a Fever, at that Time a Lodger in his House; the Doctor took the Opportunity of prescribing Matrimony to her, as a Specifick which he was sure would compleat her cure; and on consenting to take his advice in it, they were married at her late Brother's Plantation" (*CRG*, 4:526-27).

Anne inherited her brother's estate in Joseph's Town including the 500-acre Savannah River plantation Mulberry Grove. Under Cuthbert it was a great success; under the diligent attention of Graham it flourished. He raised and sold mulberry seedlings for Georgia's fledgling silk industry, experimented with raising cotton and rice, cut and sold timber to the lumber yards. In 1752 the Trustees granted to Patrick Graham and his brother David adjoining tracts of 450 acres and 500 acres, respectively, which they called Redford for their home in Scotland. William Stephens noted that Graham was "a Man generally well esteemd among us All but that gave up his apothecary practice after his marriage" (*CRG*, 24:418-19).

Graham died 30 May 1755. Heirs included his widow and relatives in Scotland to whom he left property in Georgia as well as "lands in Redford in the Shire of Perth in North Britain." In 1758 his widow married South Carolina planter James Bulloch. Egmont, *Journal*, 153; *Early Settlers*, 76; *Conveyances C-1*, 66-67, 244-45, 263-65, 286-87, 324-25, 333; "Proceedings," 36:46-47; *CRG*, 4:526-27, 4: Suppl., 148, 5:557, 6:353, 7:9, 18; 27:97; *Colonial Wills*, 64; marriage contract, Book O, p. 150, App. 3, G-Ar; *Savannah River Plantations*, 58-64 (Mulberry Grove), 351; *Indian Affairs*, 80-81; Stephens, *Journal, 1741–1743*, 140; Stephens, *Journal, 1743–1745*, 212; Temple, *Georgia Journeys*, 290; Gay, *Medical Profession*, see index; Wilson, *Drugs and Pharmacy*, 17, 19-21, 15.

62. Daniel Demetre (d. 1758), mariner and planter, commanded the Georgia colony's ten-oared, single swivel gun scout boat *Frederica* in the early 1740s. Following disbandment of the regiment in 1749, he became master of the boat crews, each with a coxswain. The sixteen-oared *Hanover* and the ten-oared *Prince George*, commanded by Demetre, replaced two of the old vessels, and a third was repaired. It is very likely that *Prince George* was the armed vessel that accompanied Jonathan Bryan and his companions from St. Simons to the St. Johns River.

Three months after his trip with Bryan, the Governor and Council ordered Demetre on a secret mission to scout Amelia Island in the *Prince George* to ascertain if settlers were there contrary to the treaty between Spain and England. Despite Creek Indian reports to that effect, however, Demetre found none. Ordered south again in July 1754 he cruised within twelve miles of St. Augustine but observed no Spanish engaged in preparations for war.

Through grants and purchase Demetre acquired considerable property—some 1,400 acres in the Newport District and on Sapelo Island plus town, garden, and farm lots in Savannah and Hardwick. On 2 April 1752 he signed a marriage agreement with Ann (Cassell) Harris, the daughter of Anna Cassell Salter and widow of William Harris. Ann inherited lands from her mother, her stepfather Thomas Salter, and Thomas Pratt. Daniel Demetre signed his will in Savannah on 12 July (proved 10 August 1758), mentioning his 750-acre plantation "Dickenson's Neck [now Harris Neck] in the district of Sappelo and Newport," eight slaves, granddaughter Ann Harris, and a legacy in trust for the Society of Free Masons in Savannah. *CRG*, 27:84; *Council Journal, 1753–1760*, 2, 3, 8, 19; Bryant, *English Crown Grants*, 32, 33; *Council Journal, 1761–1767*, 1, 27, 30, 52, 53, 66, 103; *Entry of Claims*, 32-34; Dumont, *Colonial Georgia*, 2, 12, 22-23, 40, 122; *Colonial Wills*, 40; Jones, *History of Georgia*, 1:426-27.

63. William Simmons's intended settlement on 1,000 acres along the Newport River was presumably on land that in 1758 became the two parishes of St. Andrews and St. John, separated by the river. Neither he nor this settlement has been identified. It may be significant, however, that in August 1752 an Elizabeth Simmons was allotted 400 acres by the President and Assistants in Georgia, and on 6 July 1757 John Graves applied for 1,000 acres between South Newport and "Bind Swamp" [Bird Swamp?] on behalf of his daughter-in-law (possibly stepchild) Elizabeth Simmons, who had eighteen slaves "now in the Province" (*Council Journal, 1753–1760*, 54). The Council approved 500 acres. On 2 October 1759 the Council granted to Elizabeth Simmons 500 acres in the Midway District. An Elizabeth Simmons was deeded lot no. 90 in Sunbury (undated), and Midway Church records indicate that an Elizabeth Simmons died in 1765, but no probate record for her has been found.

The following may be useful for further research: On 18 January 1722 the will of planter John Simmons, Jr., of Berkeley County, South Carolina, named his sons William, John, and Thomas Simmons. In Colleton County, South Carolina, on 8 March 1748/1749, planter Thomas Simmons signed his will and mentioned wife, Elizabeth; unmarried daughter Elizabeth (under twenty-one years); and his brother William Simmons. One William Simmons, planter of Prince William Parish, Granville County, South Carolina, signed his will 17 March 1755, proved 11 April 1755. Among those mentioned were his wife, Sarah; son John (not yet nineteen); niece Elizabeth ("daughter of my brother Thomas Simmons, dec'd"); nephew Thomas Bee; the Independent or Congregational Church of Christ at Stoney Creek; Jonathan Bryan of Georgia; Sarah (daughter of John Graves); and William Graves (son of William Graves) of Beech Hill, and others. *SC Wills, 1740–1760*, 82, 92, 191; *Council Journals, 1761–1767*, 23; *Georgia Memorials*, 35; *CRG*, 27:89; Stacy, *Midway*, 133; Jones, *Dead Towns*, 160.

64. William Gerard De Brahm (1718–1799), cartographer, surveyor, and engineer, was a member of Bryan's brave little southward-bound contingent until he became ill at Fort St. Andrew on Cumberland Island. He was a glamorous traveling companion. Born in Germany, De Brahm trained for military life, but in 1751 he and his wife emigrated instead to Georgia. Their passage was paid by Samuel Urlsperger, Bishop of Augsberg (one of two Europeans to serve as a Trustee of the Georgia colony), in exchange for which De Brahm was put in charge of a group of German-speaking Protestants who settled at Ebenezer. On arrival he worked as a commercial agent for Trustee Christian von Münch, an Augsburg banker and a close associate of the bishop. Pastor Johann Martin Boltzius mentioned "von Brahm" going up to survey the Savannah River and "to view the much praised land at Bryar's Creek for a settlement either to himself and Mr. Von Munch" (*CRG*, 26:311). Apparently, soon after arriving in Georgia he began signing his name De Brahm instead of Von Brahm. Because of his training as a military engineer, his strong interest in philosophy, natural history, and cartography, De Brahm caught the attention of the governing bodies of both South Carolina and Georgia. In Charleston he oversaw construction of the city's fortifications; his first effort in Georgia was a map of the Georgia coast from Savannah to St. Catherines in 1752.

By 1753–1754 he actively sought land in Georgia. At the time he petitioned for a grant in Savannah, he also solicited subscriptions for a map of South Carolina and Georgia in the *South-Carolina Gazette*, 23 October 1752. It is tempting to think that during the summer of 1753 Bryan invited the distinguished engineer on his "Voyage of . . . Discovery and Observations" in order to further De Brahm's work on his new map. In 1754 the royal government appointed De Brahm and Henry Yonge the first two surveyors-general of Georgia. Two years later De Brahm became embroiled in a heated disagreement with Capt. Raymond Demere over the plans, site, and construction of the ill-fated Fort Loudoun in what is now Tennessee. De Brahm returned to Georgia and was instrumental in planning fortifications for the defense of the colony; in 1765 he moved to East Florida where he served as surveyor-general of the Southern District. Six years later he was recalled to London because of charges stemming from his feud with the royal governor. Once exonerated in 1775, De Brahm expected to continue his surveys in the south only to arrive in Charleston at the outbreak of the American Revolution and face imprisonment as a loyal British subject. Eventually permitted to leave for Europe, he spent the duration of the war in France and England. On returning to America in 1791 he resided near Philadelphia, and it was at his home Bellair that he died in 1799. For biographical details of his life see the introduction by Louis De Vorsey, Jr., in De Brahm, *Report*, 3-59, 262 n. 22. See also *DGB*, 1:246-48; Wilson, "Missing Salzburger Diaries"; *Council Journal, 1753–1760*; *Council Journal, 1761–1767*; *CRG*, 27:88; and *Georgia Memorials*; Jones, *Georgia Dutch*, 146, 158-61.

65. John Williamson, Jr. (ca. 1730–1766), planter, was the son of John and Mary (Bower) Williamson of Beaver Plantation, Colleton County, South Carolina; he was also Jonathan Bryan's brother-in-law. From his father's estate in 1733 young John inherited land at "Spoons adjoining Benjamin Williamson" (*SC Wills, 1670–1740*, 192). In 1742 he inherited £1,000 from his mother's kinsman, Edward Hext of Charles Town, South Carolina. On 11 September 1755 John Williamson, then of Prince William Parish, married Magdelene Postell in St. Helena Parish. He evidently moved to Georgia or planned to move in 1758, because the following year the Council granted him 100 acres on the "Savannah River the upper part of the Long Reach" (*Council Journal, 1753–1760*, 136). Col. Isaac Hayne noted Williamson's death on 22 February 1766. The court cited Magdalen [*sic*] Williamson and Andrew Postel [*sic*] to administer the estate in Prince William Parish on 14 May 1766.

Mary (Bower) Williamson, John's widowed mother, married Jonathan Bryan's brother Joseph Bryan (1722–1788) on 13 October 1737. She died in 1776, leaving part of her estate to the children of her deceased son John Williamson; her daughter-in-law Magdalen [*sic*] Williamson was one of the executors. *SCHGM* 6:31 n. 7; 9 (1908): 122-23; 10 (1909): 163; 23 (1922): 81, 148, 163, 201; *Colonial Wills*, 20-21; *SC Wills, 1740–60*, 9-10 (will of Edward Hext); Dumont, *Colonial Georgia*, 19; Salley, *Register of St. Philips's Parish*, 169. See also *Savannah River Plantations*; Gallay, *Planter Elite*.

66. This site (in what is now Bryan County, Georgia) was referred to as the Elbow, then named George-Town in 1754, and a year later renamed Hardwicke in honor of Philip Yorke (1690–1764), First Earl of Hardwicke, the Lord Chancellor. Gov. John Reynolds considered it "the only fit place for the capital" of Georgia and requested funds for constructing public buildings. The town was laid out and lots were granted—Bryan himself acquired lot 47 in 1755—but the British government neglected to support the

enterprise, and it never became more than a small trading village although various attempts were made to revive interest in its development as late as 1866. In 1878 Jones included Hardwick [*sic*] in his *Dead Towns of Georgia*, 224-32. An exact-plan of George-Town so named by Patrick Graham, Esqr., president of the Province of George, in honr. to His Royal Highness George, Prince of Wales, &ca. Surveyed & delineated by order of the President & Council of Georgia, this 9th day of May 1754, by Henry Yonge, survy. [1754], manuscript, Geography and Map Division, DLC; *CRG*, 7:101, 27:63, 103-104; *Council Journal, 1753–1760*, 20; Stevens, *History of Georgia*, 1:405-406, 433, 2:19; *DNB*.

67. St. Catherines Island was reserved for Creek tribal use under the treaties and understandings reached in 1733, 1735, 1736, and 1739 between Oglethorpe and the Indians, and in April 1744 all the Yamacraw Indians who lived in a village near Savannah moved to the island. The following year they had several plantations of corn, and visitor Edward Kimber found on the island the "most fruitful Soil, and . . . [with] larger Tracts of open Land than any I have observed, and to abound in all Kinds of Game, on which the good *Indians* regaled us." Probably some of the Yamacraw moved there to raise cattle.

Thomas Bosomworth (?–1783), brother of Adam, was on St. Catherines by March 1746 (at the latest) with six slaves and herds of cattle that he bought on credit in South Carolina. His creditors obviously saw this as a good investment, but the illegal slaves surprised and angered the Trustees. Bosomworth's activity, raising livestock, was not an infringement on St. Catherines since the Indians understood tribal land to be "common property." Mary Musgrove (ca. 1700–1766), Bosomworth's half-Indian wife, was an important figure among the Creeks and would have assumed her right to run cattle the same as any other Creek. This contrasts with Coulter's perception of the couple as "land pirates" and Bosomworth's aspiration to be a "cattle king."

It is curious that Bryan made no mention of Spanish mission ruins on St. Catherines, described in 1687 by Dunlop as a "great Setlement" with the "ruins of several houses" deserted by the Spanish "for ffear of the English about 3 years agoe" ("Dunlop's Voyage," 131). Perhaps they were obscured by the overgrowth of vegetation in 1753. Recent archaeological excavations on the island uncovered what is to date the largest collection of Spanish mission artifacts in America. Juricek, *Georgia Treaties*, 132-33; Louis De Vorsey, Jr., "Indian Boundaries in Colonial Georgia," *GHQ* 54 (1970): 68-78 (p. 68 n. 12 cites unpublished CRG 33, typescript MS on microfilm, University of Georgia Libraries); Kimber, *Observations*, 14; "Dunlop's Voyage," 131; Hemperley, *Georgia's Boundaries*, 46-47; Stephens, *Journal, 1743–1745*, 95-96; Fisher, "Mary Musgrove," 416; Coulter, "Mary Musgrove, 'Queen of the Creeks': A Chapter of Early Georgia Troubles," *GHQ* 11 (1927): 13-14; *DGB*, 1:96-98; Thomas, *St. Catherine*.

68. Adam Bosomworth (?–1765), is among those listed in James Oglethorpe's Regiment along with Abraham and Thomas Bosomworth, and he evidently received a land grant in 1749. Styling himself "Gentleman" with no occupation noted, Adam was the designated attorney for his brother Thomas in two deeds dated 11 March 1750. In December 1756, as the owner of thirteen slaves, he requested a grant of 500 acres on the North Newport River, St. John Parish. In May 1759 the Council granted him an additional 300 acres, and his wife, Elizabeth, a 500-acre tract in the same parish.

Adam Bosomworth married Elizabeth Maxwell, a daughter of James and Mary Maxwell (possibly their daughter Elizabeth born 2 July 1725 in St. Thomas and St. Dennis Parish, South Carolina). On 18 March 1765, between Midway muster-field and Kenneth Baillie's, Bosomworth was "thrown from his horse against a tree" and killed (*Ga Gaz*, 28 March 1765); his widow was sole heir and executrix of his estate. She married Thomas Young (ca. 1734–1808) on 20 October 1765 at Southampton, near Sunbury. A native of Scotland, he arrived in Georgia about 1758; claiming a wife and 47 slaves in 1767, Young received a grant of 300 acres adjacent to the Adam Bosomworth property. Under provisions of her mother's will, Elizabeth Young inherited twenty-one slaves in 1775.

Thomas Young died 7 November 1808, aged seventy-four, a Georgia resident for fifty years. (Gravestone indicates he was in his fifty-sixth year, evidently an error.) Elizabeth Young (Eliza Ruth on gravestone) died 19 June 1814, in her eighty-sixth year, for sixty years a resident of Georgia. (If the latter is accurate she was neither Elizabeth Maxwell, daughter of James, who was born in 1725, nor a resident of Georgia at the time of Bryan's 1753 visit. It is possible that her parents named her for a sibling who died in infancy.) Both the Youngs were buried in Savannah's Colonial Cemetery. *Conveyances C-1*, 16-17, 22-23; *Council Journal, 1753–1760*, 67, 131; *Colonial Wills*, 15; *Ga Gaz*, 31 October 1765; *CMSA*, 11 November 1808; Clute, *St. Thomas and St. Denis Parish*, 36; will of Thomas Young, Chatham County, Georgia, Will Book E, p. 59; *Savannah River Plantations*, 357-60; *Savannah Republican*, 25 June 1814; *Early Epitaphs*, 198, 200; *Colonial Wills*, 92-93; Wilson, *Liberty County*, 47; *Revolutionary Records*, 1:611-17, 2:558-59; 3:373; Coldham, *American Loyalists Claims*, 546-47.

69. Live oak (*Quercus virginiana*), a magnificent semi-evergreen tree, is unique to the South. Given adequate space a single branch can span seventy-feet and shade a sizable area, hence the appreciative comments in this journal. Although difficult to work, live oak was otherwise ideally suited as a shipbuilding timber, especially for frames, knees, and other compass pieces. Extremely dense and heavy with great tensile strength and resistance to rot, its natural curves eliminated the necessity of making cross-grain cuts; its durability, as compared with other native timber, was lauded in the colonial era. Wood, *Live Oaking*; Fleetwood, *Tidecraft*, see index.

70. There is no longer a Newport River per se, but the present-day North Newport River is navigable for twenty-six miles, and the South Newport River is navigable for twenty miles, obviously neither as extensive as Bryan indicated. De Brahm's 1752 and 1757 maps depict a Serpent or Newport River. If the group traversed this well-named "Serpent River," Bryan could quite easily have thought it forty miles, considering the time required to tack or the labor to row throughout its twists and turns to reach their destination. No settlement is indicated at its headwaters, but marked on the map are three places designated Fresh Water Bluff, Indian Camp Bluff, and Benjehovah Bluff. De Brahm, *Map* (1757). For river milage see the untitled list of rivers in Georgia, U.S. Army Corps of Engineers, Savannah office (n.d.).

71. In 1772 William De Brahm wrote that in 1753 he saw on an island called Demetrius "many ruins of ancient houses" surrounded by the remains of an entrenchment one and a quarter miles in length. It seems likely that he saw these mystifying structures while traveling with Jonathan Bryan, but the date is not verifiable, because two days, 16–17 August (Thursday and Friday), are missing from Bryan's journal. On 15 August Bryan's party was apparently preparing to leave William Simmons's settlement at the head of the Serpent or Newport River. The next journal entry, dated 18 August, notes that they arose at 5 A.M. and proceeded up "river"; that afternoon they saw Sapelo Island and an "Old Spanish Fort." They lay by all night (presumably near the island) and on the following day (19 August) entered Doboy Sound.

Although he recognized the ruins on Demetrius Island as evidence of a settlement prior to 1600, De Brahm thought it was "not a Spanish outpost." Instead, he suggested that a lost group of disgruntled settlers, perhaps neither Spanish nor English, had created it. Actually, when De Brahm saw this in 1753 it was called John Smiths Island; it became known as Demetrius Island after it was granted by the Council to Daniel Demetre in 1756. Known in later decades as Creightons Island, it lies within the vast marshes bordering the Sapelo River and is adjacent to Sapelo Island. It is about two-and-a-half miles long with 1,200 to 1,500 acres of habitable land. After the last of the friars left Demetrius, Indian occupation could easily have continued for sixty or eighty years. More modern research suggests, however, that perhaps De Brahm saw ruins on Demetrius Bluff (now known as Harris Neck), a highly visible bluff on the mainland. Currently, archaeologists wonder if the as-yet-undiscovered ruins of San Miguel de Guadalpe, a lost Spanish colony, may lie in coastal Georgia, probably near Sapelo Sound. San Miguel was a full-blown Spanish settlement, "geared up for the long term," with Spaniards and Hispañolans, some married with families, black slaves, Indian slave interpreters, secular clergy, surgeons, and Dominican friars. The editors suggest that the missing pages of Bryan's journal may have included references to the ruins. If, by proceeding "up river" Bryan meant "up the Sapelo River," his group would have passed Demetrius Bluff. De Brahm's *Report on Georgia*

(1772), dedicated to the Lords Commissioners of Trade and Plantations, is cited in De Brahm, *Report*, 147; *Disputed Ruins*, 21-24; David Hurst Thomas, "Georgian Genesis: The Intercultural Beginnings," in *Georgia Humanities Lecture* (Atlanta: Georgia Humanities Council, 1993), 9; De Vorsey, "Early Maps," 18-21; Mary R. Bullard, telephone interview with Dr. Frederick C. Marland, Darien, Georgia, 28 March 1994.

72. Several branches of clan Mackintosh (or McIntosh) from the Scottish Highlands were among those who agreed to settle in Georgia in 1736/1737. They named Darien in honor of their countrymen who perished in the Darien settlement on the Isthmus of Panama in 1697. Darien, Georgia, is now the county seat of McIntosh County, which, in turn, was named in honor of the colonial McIntosh family. Egmont, *Journal*, 217; Sullivan, *McIntosh County*, 16-23.

73. Sapelo Island, in the Province of Guale, was important to Spanish interests as they endeavored to protect their sea routes between Mexico and Europe and to Christianize the Indians of *La Florida*. It is possible there was more than one mission on the island. In any case, they established a Franciscan mission, probably sometime prior to 1597, for in that year the Guale Indians staged a major rebellion against the priests. The Spanish regained control, however, and in his *Relación* of 1616 Father Luis Geronimo de Oré mentioned a visit to the "convent of San José de Zápela," by then a center for Franciscan activity in the entire province. There were still some fifty "men, children and women and pagans" who comprised the mission in 1675.

The year 1670, however, saw the establishment of the English settlement of San Jorge. Its fortifications, located at what soon came to be called Charles Town, immediately attracted Spanish and Indian attention. By 1680 Spanish authorities, recognizing their inability to protect the four Sapelo missions, began urging their removal further southward, although the Christianized Sapelo Indians indicated their preference for suicide rather than relocation. Even while relocation was being discussed, assaults from the sea brought Sapelo's missions to their end. Late in the spring of 1683 the French pirate Grammont sailed northward from St. Augustine to attack the coastal missions. In 1684, "unknown to the residents of Guale, . . . a group of some 11 pirate ships had united off the west coast of Florida and decided to mount yet another assault on St. Augustine" (Worth, *Georgia Coast*, 40). Although the pirate fleet was scattered by a storm, a remnant led by a pirate known as Thomas Jingle slipped further northward in October to raid the Sea Islands for provisions. By the end of that month most of the mission population of Sapelo had hurriedly evacuated. English-allied Yamassee Indians reoccupied it by the following March (1685). The settlement was razed by the Spanish captain Francisco de Fuentes in a retaliatory attack of 1686.

During a visit there on 29 April 1687, Captain Dunlop wrote: "we came about noon to Sapale [*sic*] to very large plantations where we see the ruins of houses burned by the

Spaniards themselves We see the Vestiges of a ffort; many great Orange Trees cut down by the Spaniards in septr last There was great plenty of ffigs peaches; Artechocks onions etc. growing in the preists garden his house had been of Brick & his small chappell, but all had been burned to Ashes last harvest by themselves; we see the remains & rags of old clothes wch. [which] some of our people know to have belongd to the Inhabitants of port Royall" ("Dunlop's Voyage," 131-32).

Indian agriculturists may have continued to cultivate the mission gardens, because traces of sea-island gardens and orchards remained. In July 1721 when Col. John Barnwell arrived to construct Fort King George on the English-Spanish frontier at the mouth of the Altamaha River, his men put ashore at Sapelo where they gathered "Spanish garlick & . . . figs," but he mentioned no fortification ("Barnwell's Journal," 196). Some twenty years later British soldiers and settlers arriving on the island referred to a "Spanish fort" and a garden with oranges and limes at the extreme northeast corner. William De Brahm's 1760 map of Sapelo depicts such a garden in this area and also notes a "Spanish Fort."

For over a century historians and archaeologists have investigated and written about Sapelo's "Spanish fort," but so far the mission site has not been located. Archaeologists currently believe that the site of Mission San Joseph de Sápala is almost without question situated at Bourbon Field, on the northern end of Sapelo Island. De Brahm, like most of the English, knowing there was once a fort, undoubtedly confused the 4,000-year-old Sapelo Island shell ring with such a structure.

For mission building, see Thomas, "Saints and Soldiers," 94-116. For archaeological reviews: Larson, Spanish on Sapelo," 35-45, 66; Larson, *Sapelo Island*, 6; De Brahm and Yonge, "A Plan of the Islands of Sappola," surveyed for Grey Elliot (1760), GU-HR, reproduced in Sullivan, *McIntosh County*, 51. For the end of Mission San Joseph de Sapala (1684): Worth, *Georgia Coast*, 40-46. Also personal communication, John E. Worth to Virginia S. Wood, 1 November 1994.

74. Oglethorpe named Jekyll Island (hence Jekyll Sound) in honor of his friend Sir Joseph Jekyll (1663–1738), a distinguished lawyer and statesman. He and his wife contributed £600 toward establishing the Georgia colony. *CRG*, 1:122; *Oglethorpe's Georgia*, 1:345; *DNB*.

75. Frederica, St. Simons Island, was one of two garrisoned towns south of Savannah planned by Oglethorpe to thwart Spanish aggression. It was settled by the English and by German Salzburgers, and the first group arrived in February 1736. See Ivers, *British Drums*, 51-52.

76. Darien was the other fortified town that Oglethorpe planned as protection against incursions from the Spanish. Recruited in the vicinity of Inverness, Scotland, a group of Highlanders agreed to become settlers and, including their families, 177 arrived in Georgia

in early January 1735/1736. They built their town and garrison adjacent to the Altamaha River about a mile from the site of old Fort King George. Egmont, *Journal*, 147, 156, 309; Ivers, *British Drums*, 9, 51; Cook, *Fort King George*.

77. In this context a freshet is a flood or overflowing river caused by heavy rains.

78. This was probably William Abbott or Abbot (living 1761), woodcutter of Goswell Street in London, who embarked for Georgia under the Trustee's charge, arriving in the colony during February 1735/1736 along with his mother, Elizabeth Baldwyn, and his servant, Richard Hart. The Trustees granted Abbot a lot in Frederica, where he was appointed second constable "in case of vacancy" on 26 September 1735. During the 1740s he was keeper of the King's Magazine at Fort Frederica; he was a turner; he unloaded transports and searched for slaves; and he delivered messages to Oglethorpe during the expedition to Florida in 1742. In carrying out his duties as constable, Abbott was involved in a dispute between two factions in 1745: the civil authority and certain individuals who engaged in illegal trade with the Spanish in St. Augustine. As constable he took an inventory of supplies left at Frederica by the disbanded regiment in 1749. Seven years later during King George's War, Abbott was in the Caribbean when the Spanish schooner in which he was a passenger (Cuba to Jamaica) was captured by privateer Richard Haddon of New York, who, claiming she was French, illegally plundered the vessel. He then took passengers Abbott and Henry Myerhoffer, also a Georgia resident, to Jamaica and held them in close confinement at Lucea for fifteen days until his schooner was fitted out for sea. By June 1761 Abbott was back in Georgia where he attested to the validity of a document before a justice of the peace in Savannah. *Early Georgia Settlers*, 1, 3, 22; Kimber, *Expedition*, 19; *CRG*, 1:242, 2:11, 130; 3:108; 6:210, 241, 252; 7:242; 21:260, 26:37; *Conveyances J*, 213; Egmont, *Journal*, 113; *Conveyances C-1*, 43; Libel of Richard Haddon, Case File #187, Admiralty Case Files, U.S. Dist. Courts for the Southern Dist. of New York, Records of the Dist. Courts of the U.S., RG21, DNA, Northeast Region, New York NY. Transcripts of the documents in case file #187 were published in Jameson, *Privateering and Piracy*, 537-66.

79. Raymond Demere (d. 1766), military officer, planter, and merchant, a native of France, served for ten years with the British Army and was among the troops at Gibraltar before joining Oglethorpe's Regiment on 30 September 1738. He was commissioned a captain-lieutenant on 12 May 1741 and captain of the regiment's 5th Company on 31 January 1742. Demere's knowledge of Spanish made him a valuable asset, and both Oglethorpe and the South Carolina governor relied on him as an emissary to the Spanish governor at St. Augustine. For his military involvement during the battles of July 1742 on St. Simons, see Ivers, *British Drums*, 163-67.

After disbandment of Oglethorpe's Regiment in 1749, Demere remained with the Independent Companies of South Carolina as a company commander. In November 1753 at Keowee, he witnessed the agreement between Gov. John Glen and the Cherokee Nation for the Fort Prince George tract. During 1754–1755 he had certain responsibilities for the detachments stationed on St. Simons, Jekyll, and Cumberland Islands. In 1756 Demere was sent to build and garrison the ill-fated Fort Loudoun on the Tennessee River, plans for which were drawn by William De Brahm. Both men were in poor health at the time, which probably acerbated the conflict that erupted between them over both site and plans for the fortification. At Raymond Demere's request in 1757 his command at Fort Loudoun was assigned to his younger brother, Capt. Paul Demere, who was killed by Indians following capitulation of the fort in 1760. Raymond Demere was subsequently on duty in South Carolina's Indian country constructing forts.

A sociable individual, Demere was an active member of "the Club" at Frederica, a group of officers who took turns dining together each evening in their houses. Philadelphia visitors William Logan and James Pemberton joined this group on a number of occasions in 1745/1746. On returning from Fort Loudoun Demere resided at Frederica in his brother's house, but a disastrous fire on 9 April 1758 swept through town and destroyed most of the buildings. Of his own losses Demere wrote that his "house was burnt with everything about it and nothing but my Cloaths and some little Plate was saved" (Demere to Mongomery [*sic*]). On selling his commission in 1761 he settled into the life of a Frederica merchant. His residence was about a mile away on a fifty-acre tract granted to him by Oglethorpe and named for his former commander, Col. William Stanhope (later general), First Earl of Harrington. Thomas Spalding grew up on St. Simons and recalled Demere as "one of the oldest officers of the Regiment. [He] was a French Huguenot of considerable fortune, much of which he expended in ornamenting a country seat, rather in the French taste. . . . At Harrington Hall, the seat of Captain Demere, the enclosures were entirely of orange or cassina, a species of Ilex, but the most beautiful of the family" (*CGHS*, 1:274).

In addition to lots in Frederica and Hardwicke, Demere obtained grants of hundreds of acres in outlying areas including 600 acres on Jekyll Island in 1765, but he died a year later. His will was probated 26 June 1766. *Davis* v. *Demere*, Raymond Demere Papers, Duke University, transcripts and photocopies in the Hartridge Coll.; Rayd. Demere to Coll. Mongomery [Col. Archibald Montgomerie], 30 April 1758, William Henry Lylleton Papers, William L. Clements Library, University of Michigan; *CRG*, 5:97; 22, Pt. 2:232; 27:82; Logan, "Journal," 172, 175, 176; Margaret Davis Cate, "The Demere Brothers— Raymond and Paul," n.d., unpublished MS, Cate Coll.; *DNB*, 18:927-31; De Brahm, *Report*, 19-24; Williams, "British-American Officers," 188, 191, 293-95; Clark, *Colonial Soldiers*, 974, 977-78, 982, 994-96, 1007; Dumont, *Colonial Georgia*, 25, 38, 45; *Entry of Claims*, 30, 139; *Conveyances C-1*, 99-100, 194-96; *Conveyances J*, 104, 109-10. See also *Council Journal, 1753–1760*; *Council Journal, 1761–1767*; *Georgia Memorials*; *Indian Affairs*, 519-20; Hamer, "Anglo-French Rivalry" and "Fort Loudoun"; *Colonial Wills*, 39-40.

80. This was probably James Penny or Penney (living 1764), a sergeant on the muster roll of Capt. Raymond Demere's Company of Independent Foot, 1754, and a corporal in the Second Troop of Georgia Rangers under Capt. James Edward Powell, 1764. In 1754 Penny and Lt. Thomas Goldsmith became involved in a legal action brought by privateer Caleb Davis who accused them of obstructing Constable William Abbot from executing his duty in the case of *Davis* v. *Demere*. Evidently Penny failed as a merchant in Frederica, for on 30 March 1758 he assigned a power of attorney to his creditor Raymond Demere. The debt amounted to £1,577, and the court awarded Demere all of Penny's slaves, livestock, and all other goods and chattels. Raymond Demere Papers, Duke University, with transcripts and copies in the Hartridge Coll.; Clark, *Colonial Soldiers*, 191, 995, 1063-64; *Conveyances C-1*, 99-100; *Conveyances J*, 110.

81. Punch originated in India some 2,000 years ago, and merchants of the East India Company introduced it into Britain during the seventeenth century. The name itself, derived from a Hindu word meaning five, refers to the ingredients: "sugar, spirits, citron juice, water, aromatic flavorings" (Wilson, 401). Despite the prohibition against selling and consuming rum in the early days of settlement, many of the Georgia colonists imbibed. This practice greatly agitated Oglethorpe who, in 1734, attributed their "petulancy," disobedience, intemperance, and illnesses to rum punch. A decade later, its popularity unabated, punch was offered to William Logan on several occasions in Frederica. Wilson, *Food & Drink*, 401; Temple, *Georgia Journeys*, 24-26; Logan, "Journal," 167, 175, 177.

82. English settlers planted these orange trees. In 1743 Edward Kimber saw them growing along Frederica's "several spacious streets" and predicted that in the near future they would "render the Town pleasingly shady." Maj. William Horton reportedly planted 10,000 orange trees in rows on his Jekyll Island property. Both Oglethorpe and Horton may have planted the calamondin, hardiest of all citrus hybrids grown in America. Unsurpassed for making punch and other beverages, it is bright orange in color and remains on the tree throughout the winter months. Kimber, *Observations* 6; Bailey, *Hortus Third*, 279.

83. The need for a good fort on St. Simons was expressed as early as 1722 in the South Carolina Commons House of Assembly. In 1736 Oglethorpe ordered the construction of two adjacent fortifications at the southern tip of St. Simons Island overlooking the sound. The first, Delegal's Fort, consisted of a blockhouse with three field cannons and was named for its first commander, Lt. Philip Delegal. An earthworks called Fort St.

Simons was prepared approximately 1,200 feet to the west. It had seven field cannons, and five additional cannons were positioned between the two forts. Behind them were huts for the soldiers and their families. To link these fortifications with Fort Frederica, seven miles to the northeast, Oglethorpe had a military road cut through the woods. During the Spanish invasion of July 1742, the enemy destroyed both installations at the island's south end.

On this site in 1871 the U.S. government constructed a lighthouse and keeper's cottage that is now a part of the Coastal Georgia Historical Society and Museum of Coastal History. "Barnwell's Journal," 192; *CRG* 31:78, 445; *Gentleman's Magazine* (1739): 22-23; *CGHS*, 1:181, 261, 2:82, 4:9, 7:Pt. 3, 72- 95; Cate, "Fort Frederica," 123-24.

84. William Horton (1702–1748), "subsheriff of Herefordshire," who became a military officer and planter, paid his own way to Georgia and arrived in February 1735/1736 in the ship *Symmonds*, along with John and Charles Wesley. He was Col. James Oglethorpe's Ensign in the 42nd Regiment of Foot in 1737; in October 1738 Horton was promoted to lieutenant in the Fifth Company. That same month Oglethorpe informed the Trustees that "the Storehouse at Savannah has supported this division Providence so ill that the people must have starved or abandoned the place had not Mr Horton given them his own cattle & corn to eat" (*CRG*, 22: Pt. 1, 275-76). Oglethorpe sent Horton to England to recruit thirty men for the regiment in 1739; by May 1740 he was captain of the Grenadier Company that was added to Oglethorpe's regiment. When the latter left Georgia in April 1743, Horton (by then a major) became commander-in-chief of the military force stationed at Frederica.

Within the year of his arrival in Georgia the Trustees granted Horton 500 acres on Jekyll Island, where he built a house on what is now DuBignon Creek. Retreating Spanish soldiers destroyed his house and cattle after the invasion of 1742, but recent archaeological excavations establish that a second house was constructed on charred remains of the first. Tabby walls of this second structure still exist.

In the autumn of 1745 at Frederica, Philadelphia merchants William Logan and James Pemberton spent a good deal of time with Horton and found him genial company. Logan commented that "Capt Horton supplies all Frederica with Fresh Meat," and on a visit to Jekyll they strolled to Horton's barley field "which [the major] has With the utmost Industry got into fine Ordr. and sowed and was just come up & looked Well" (Logan, "Journal," 172, 177). The following year John Pye remarked that Horton had "a very Large Barnfull of Barley not inferior to ye Barley in England, about 20 Ton of Hay in one Stack, a spacious House & Fine Garden, a plow was going wth. Eight Horses, And above all I saw Eight Acres of Indigo of which he has made a good Quantity" (*CRG*, 25:97). Bryan's description of Horton's house and outbuildings is apparently the most detailed of the period.

Horton maintained close ties with South Carolina, where he had business dealings with Henry Laurens, and although a Georgia resident, he was elected in 1747 to represent St. Helena Parish in South Carolina's Commons House of Assembly. Shortly thereafter, at age forty-two, he died between August and December 1748 "to the universal sorrow of all his Acquaintance" (Stephens, *CRG* 25:365). He was buried inside Savannah's Christ Church. The following year the government awarded his widow, Rebecca, an annual pension of £30, which ceased in 1800. Between 1749 and 1766 Jekyll Island was a military reservation commanded by Capt. Raymond Demere, and it was under these circumstances that Bryan made his visit there in 1753. Years later, in 1803, Levi Sheftall recalled Horton as a tall man with red hair and identified the major's burial place in Savannah. His remains were discovered and identified in 1803 when work was being done on the foundation of Christ Church. *Early Settlers*, 79; *Conveyances C-1*, 137; Stephens, *Journal, 1743-1745*, 218-19; *CRG*, 5:659, 687; 12:275-76; 36:41; Kimber, *Expedition*, n. 7; British Pension Register Indexes 8227, 8229, abstracts in Horton file, Hartridge Coll.; Williams, "British-American Officers," 188, 189, 190, 193, 195; Clark, *Colonial Soldiers*, 974, 977-78, 985; *BDSC*, 335; Egmont, *Journal*, 109, 276, 293, 320; Juricek, *Georgia Treaties*; Logan, "Journal," 166-79; Stephens, *Journal 1741–1743, 1743–1745*, see index; *Laurens Papers*, see index; Fauber, "Comprehensive Report"; Ruple, "Horton House"; Stern, "Sheftall Diaries," 271. See also Ivers, *British Drums*; *Privy Council*, 4:128-30.

85. British settlers viewed the barrier islands as potential horse farms, and in this context Oglethorpe called attention to Amelia and Cumberland Islands in 1736. Having left a stud of the Trust's horses and mares on those islands, he wrote, "when I went last for England . . . the colts bred out of them are very good." "Oglethorpe's Discourse," 132 (11 October 1739).

86. Mark Carr (d. 1767), military officer, planter, and founder of Sunbury, Georgia, served in England as quartermaster in a regiment of dragoons, the Scotch Greys. In 1729 at Doncaster, York, he married Jane Perkins, daughter of apothecary Roger Perkins. Jane subsequently "deserted her husband and went to reside in Paris." In 1738 Carr joined Oglethorpe's regiment, embarked for Georgia on the transport *Union*, "and took his three children with him" (Petition of William Carr). He became captain of the Marine Company of Boatmen.

Oglethorpe granted Carr a 500-acre tract in 1739 that he developed as Hermitage plantation (now Hermitage Island some 4.5 miles north of Brunswick). The following year Oglethorpe sent Carr on a recruiting mission for the new Marine Company, and during his six-month absence a guard of regulars was assigned to his plantation. On 18 March 1741 a "Party of *Spanish Indians* [Yamassee] from *Augustina*" [attacked] . . . before dawn, killed several soldiers and servants, wounded others, locked the Women and

Children in a Cellar, Pillaged the House," and made off with the booty in Carr's boat but was later apprehended (*CRG*, Supplement, 4:117).

Returning in 1741 with new recruits from Virginia, Maryland, and South Carolina, Carr rebuilt the Hermitage including four blockhouses (Carr's Fort); in a safer location across the Turtle River he began another plantation on Blyth Island. Indians raided the Hermitage a second time in 1744, as reported in distant Philadelphia, but the perpetrators were caught as they had been previously. Col. Alexander Heron favorably compared Carr's 1,000 acres at Plug Point plantation (now part of the city of Brunswick) to those in Virginia. He produced excellent tobacco, and in 1742 Carr's fields also yielded 1,200 bushels of corn. William Logan visited two of Carr's plantations where he found "as fine a Qty. of Cattle" as he had ever seen. Both Logan and his cousin James Pemberton enjoyed the captain's hospitality in 1745 and 1746.

Mark Carr participated in the Battle of Bloody Marsh on St. Simons and in subsequent military actions commanded by Oglethorpe. Maj. William Horton appointed him Judge of the Vice-Admiralty Court in 1745 at Frederica; in 1755 he was a member of the Georgia Assembly; and he continued to receive large grants of land including an island at Midway and a tract known as Fish Hawk Nest Ponds on St. Simons. On 15 June 1758, the same year that his Sunbury project became a reality, he was commissioned a colonel. Less than a decade later, in December 1767, he drowned in the Turtle River. His will, signed 8 June 1767, devised all property to his children. *CRG*, 4, Supplement, 117; 6:220, 370-71; 27:81, 87; Logan, "Journal," 170-78; *Laurens Papers*, 5:288-91; Clark, *Colonial Soldiers*, 949-50, 974-75, 981, 1071; *Philadelphia Gazette*, 9 March 1744; Cate, "Fort Frederica," 125, 137, 141; *Colonial Wills*, 27; Ivers, *British Drums*, 144-46, 159, 187; Temple, *Georgia Journeys*; Cate, *Our Todays*, 160.

87. White Post, at Carteret's Point, marked a lookout on the mainland "Opposite Frederica at the Hog Crawl" (*CRG*, 9:647), where Georgia Rangers built a small fortification called Bachelor's Redoubt. It was about four miles from Frederica, and the few men stationed there communicated with the fort by the boat *Bachelor's Redoubt*. This site is located in the Marshes of Mackay, a present-day subdivision of Brunswick. Kimber, *Observations*, 6; *CRG*, 9:598, 704, 720, 779, 782; 10:598, 740; 25:468; Jones, *Dead Towns*, 123; Fred C. Cook, Brunswick, Georgia, telephone conversation with Virginia S. Wood, 1 July 1993. See also Ivers, *British Drums*, 137.

88. Opposite, in the left margin, are the words "Schooner Landing" hand lettered in pencil in a different hand and partially obscured by the property stamp of the Georgia Historical Society. The editors find no such place indicated on the *St. Andrew Sound and Satilla River National Ocean Service Chart 11504*, 13th ed. (Washington DC: National Oceanic and Atmospheric Administration, 1991).

89. When Chief of the Yamacraw Tomochichi made his first formal speech to Oglethorpe in 1735, he presented the general with a highly prized and elaborately painted buffalo skin. A few years later a puzzled Earl of Egmont dutifully recorded in his journal the chief's gift of hides to the Trustees including "6 Bouffler skins." To many colonial coastal Georgians buffalo hunting was a familiar activity. Thomas Spalding wrote that his grandfather, Col. William McIntosh (1726–1801), told him about seeing as many as "ten thousand buffaloes in a herd, between Darien and Sapelo River" (*CGHS*, 1:268). A number of geographical place names in Georgia are associated with their migrating routes and resting places, such as Buffalo Swamp (south side of the Altamaha River); Buffalo Creek (forms the headwater of Turtle River), Buffalo River (flows into Turtle River), both in Glynn County; and Buffalo Ford (south side of the Great Satilla River) in Camden County.

None of these buffalo names are known to be of Indian origin; in fact, they came into use only after the first English traders journeyed into the Carolinas and, later, into Georgia. Historians suggest that the range of buffalo extended to the southeast no earlier than 1670 or 1680. They were probably attracted to pasturage created by the aboriginal practice of "slash-and-burn" to clear land for agricultural purposes. As these fields were abandoned and covered by grasses, small herds moved to similar places in the river valleys to graze; as shrubs and trees replaced grasses the animals moved on. By the mid-eighteenth century their numbers had declined precipitously, a loss that can probably in large measure be attributed to the introduction of firearms. Egmont, *Journal*, 69; Rostlund, "Historic Bison"; Larson, *Aboriginal Subsistence*, 181-82; Baine, "Creek Pictograph," 43-52; Bartram, "Diary," 164; Catesby, *Natural History*, 4; *CRG*, 9:310, 10:290; *Oglethorpe's Letters*, 1:252; Spalding, "James Oglethorpe," 268; Cate, *Our Todays*, 225-27, 266.

90. For small eighteenth-century sailing craft and other small vessels, the Inland Passage provided a sheltered waterway extending from Massachusetts to the southern extremity of Georgia. Also called the Inland Navigation (and occasionally the Inside Route), its charts differed from ocean-going charts by including the "tidal establishment"; that is, they indicated times of high tide on days of the new or full moon at important coastal points. Today, as the Intracoastal Waterway, its Georgia section extends from Tybee Island to St. Marys [River] entrance, about 207 miles. It follows Bryan's 1753 route almost exactly except for dredged areas at certain "Narrows" and "Dividings," notably Romerly Marsh southeast of Skidaway Island between Wassaw and Ossabaw Sound; Jekyll Creek; Clubb and Plantation Creeks near Brunswick; and Skidaway Narrows. The waterway is currently used almost entirely for pleasure cruising and is under authority of the federal government. The U.S. Coast Guard has law enforcement jurisdiction and maintains all aids to navigation; the U.S. Army Corps of Engineers maintains the waterway and handles all dredging operations. It is worthwhile noting that sea level is now two or

three feet higher than it was the mid-eighteenth century. Louis De Vorsey to Virginia S. Wood, 7 March 1994; Parkman, *Waterways*, 95-112 (chronology), chart 7 (Georgia section), 82; Tinkler, *Atlantic Intracoastal Waterway*, passim.

91. Cumberland Island, twenty-two miles in length, probably had two separate settlements—one near the garrison at Fort St. Andrews and another that developed later near Fort William. Prior to the arrival of Oglethorpe's regiment, Adjutant Hugh Mackay, Jr., supervised a group of seventeen highland indentured servants who constructed a small village of huts in 1738. Located at the site of Fort St. Andrews, they were to shelter Oglethorpe's regular troops. That same year the Indian Juan Ygnacio de los Reyes described a settlement near the fort with "a number of houses, newly built and close together as in Havana, [with] a number of English women, wives of the soldiers," but he was unable to discern the exact number of dwellings. That autumn, during the mutiny at Fort St. Andrews, the frustrated mutineers ran below the fort to collect weapons at their camp called "Barrimackie." Following this incident it appears that among the married soldiers there was an important shift in living arrangements that may be attributed to the mutiny. In October 1739 Oglethorpe reported that men with wives were granted lots "which they have improved very much, particularly they have made a little village called Ballimavee, [where] there is about 24 families with good hutts built, and all have cleared and planted" (*CRG*, 35:531). Its location is a bit of a mystery. Presumably these "hutts" were similar to the soldiers' dwellings at Fort Frederica, described in this journal as "little low houses Covered with Palmettos," just as were those illustrated by von Reck in his journal.

The surgeon William Bowler mentioned "Mackays town" as his place of residence when he attended two companies of Oglethorpe's Regiment at Fort St. Andrews. It was located "7 or 8 miles from the Garrison at Cumberland" (Egmont, *Journal*, 523-24). Delivery of dispatches between the two fortifications would have been relatively rapid for a soldier on horseback riding along the horse trail running the length of the island. Logan, "Journal," 179; Ivers, *British Drums*, 80, 83-84; Serrano y Sanz, "Relación del Yndio," 261, cited in Ramsay, "Fort William"; *Von Reck's Voyage*, 74-75.

92. Fort William, situated at the south end of Cumberland Island, was about seventy miles north of St. Augustine and some forty miles south of Frederica. Built in the spring of 1740, it was a "rude quadrangular House, surrounded by Logs or Punchens, and quite unprovided for a Defence against a numerous Enemy." Following their retreat on St. Simons Island in July 1742, Spanish forces returning to Florida attacked the fort for three hours from their sailing vessels but failed to force the surrender of its fifty soldiers under Ensign Alexander Stewart. After repairs were made, Kimber wrote that by March 1742/1743 Fort William had a four pounder, some swivel guns, and "two eighteen Pounders, on a Ravelin . . . upon curious moving Platforms." This innovation, attributed to Col. William Cooke (Cook), represented a "very great improvement . . . in the manner

of mounting cannon . . . by which two men will be capable of doing as much service with such cannon as ten men with cannon mounted in the common manner" (Ramsey, 511). Referred to in 1743 as Colonel Cooke's "new invented Machine or Carriages," they were also in use at the camp battery, Fort St. Simon, and carried off by the retreating Spanish to Havana in 1743 as a "great Curiosity" (*SC Gaz*, 14 February 1743).

Fort William was in the shape of a pentagon; its ramparts of sand were twelve feet high and fifteen feet thick and supported by the above-mentioned puncheons. Bryan's allusion to effects of the 1752 hurricane appears to be unique in the annals of Georgia records and helps explain abandonment of the fort. Military detachments continued to be posted at the fort during most of 1763; it was faithfully held by a "sergeant's guard and three men" through 1765. Perhaps they performed some navigational service for sea captains unacquainted with the inlet or inland passage, in which case pilotage was probably one aspect of the fort's early history as well. It was officially abandoned in 1766. Professional archaeologists who have studied the site think its probable location was on the island's South Point. This position at the tip of a low-lying sand spit, partially stabilized by vegetation and connected to Great Cumberland by only a high sand dune, made the fortification vulnerable to erosion. They now believe that over the last 200 years Fort William has been buried under the littoral sand drift on this point.

There is some confusion among modern historians regarding the fort's proper designation. It is often referred to as "Fort Prince William" on the assumption that it was named for Prince William Augustus, Duke of Cumberland. William Ramsay asserts that documents of the period, including all of Oglethorpe's references, are unanimous in calling it simply Fort William. As early as 1757, however, map makers (including De Brahm) referred to it as "Prince Williams Fort," and ca. 1763 charts referred to adjacent waters as "Prince William Sound." Kimber, *Expedition*, nn. 8-9; Ehrenhard, "Mapping for Archaeology," 955-58; Ivers, *British Drums*, 134; Ramsey, "Fort William"; De Brahm, *Map* (1757); Wright, *Map*; Mayo, *St. Marys River*, 6-7; *Ga Gaz*, 8 December 1763, 28 March 1765.

93. The construction of Fort St. Andrews, as planned by Oglethorpe, began in April 1736 to secure the Inland Passage from Spanish forces, thereby affording some protection for Fort Frederica and the settlement at Darien. Fort St. Andrews was situated above Christmas Creek on a rise called Half Moon Bluff. Designed in the shape of a four-pointed star, the wall was an earthwork of sand and underbrush contained by a palisade of upright logs. This enclosed a powder magazine, stable, and storehouse. Adjacent to its landing was the sutler's place "which served as a combination post exchange, enlisted men's club, grocery and general store" (Bullard, *Stafford*, 194). Initially Oglethorpe ordered two companies of the regiment to be stationed at the fort. Lots were granted to the married men among them, and in 1741 about twenty-four of their families lived

several miles from the fort in "good huts" at the village they called Barriemackie or Mackays Town (Martyn). Martyn, *Impartial Inquiry*, 181; Moore, *Voyage to Georgia*, 126-27, 136; *Spanish Official Account*, 3, Pt. 3: 65-87; Bullard, *Robert Stafford*, 194-95. See also Ivers, *British Drums*, 58, 60.

94. Bryan was actually at the present-day Crooked River, but he referred to it using the Creek Indian name "Slafea-Gufea." Neither Crooked River nor Brick Hill River are real rivers, but are instead tidal creeks that form part of the dividings. A tidal phenomenon common to all barrier islands, dividings were doubtless familiar to the Frederica boatmen, and shrimp fleet Capt. Alvin Dickey, Sr., defines them as "the points where the tides reverse at slack water." In the case of the Georgia-Carolina coast, a line of barrier islands creates a series of obstacles to the tidal wave sweeping in across the ocean. This wave ignores the barrier islands, as it were, by going around each one. It splits and flows into sound or inlet at opposite ends of each island, then meets itself at a point on the far side. Because the incoming tide loses force as it reaches peak velocity, it slows down. At "slack water," usually lasting about twenty to thirty minutes, the tide ceases flowing and begins to ebb. During this period sediment transported by the tidal force is no longer held in suspension and begins falling to the bottom of the waterway. Sooner or later this deposit of sediment becomes an obstacle to navigation. The line of sedimentary deposition of this sort is often called the Dividings or the Narrows. It infuriated early boatmen on the Inland Passage who were trying to buck an ebbing tide. The various dividings behind each of the important barrier islands require periodic dredging. Frederick C. Marland, chief, Coastal Protection, Dept. of Natural Resources, State of Georgia, to Mary R. Bullard, 19 February 1982; Mary R. Bullard, personal interview with Capt. Alvin Dickey, Sr., shrimp fleet owner, Woodbine, Georgia, 1982; Parkman, *Waterways*, chap. 4. For a definition of the Cumberland Dividings, see Tinkler, *Atlantic Intercostal Waterway*, 3; Kimber, *Expedition*, 7-10; De Brahm, *Map* (1757), copies at GU-HR and Geography and Map Division, DLC.

95. *Flaflagafga*, allegedly Creek Indian for "stinking fish," is now the St. Marys River. The eastern boundary of Georgia, wrote De Brahm, reached the mouth of St. Marys, "thus called by the Spaniards, and by the Indians *Thlathlothlagupka*." He said it was a Creek Indian appellation signifying "rotten fish" (De Brahm, *History*). Actually three Indian names, *Thlathlothlagupka*, *Flaflagafga*, and *Slafea-Gufea*, are variant spellings, all standing for St. Marys River.

Jonathan Bryan gave the name *Slafea-Gufea* for Dividings River, but he was incorrect. Dividings River rarely appears on any map, one reason being that it not actually a river. The so-called Dividings "river" consists of two old, deep-water tidal creeks—Delaroche Creek and Brick Kiln River—connected to one another by a series of underwater sedimentary ridges passing through Cumberland River and its adjacent low marsh. Brick

Kiln River, if it appears at all on early charts and maps, was generally called Dividings Creek.

Bryan and his boatmen knew more about the reality of the Dividings than did contemporary cartographers. Nevertheless, even though he and his crew could pinpoint the location of the Dividings and its "river," he was in error when he gave it the Indian name for St. Marys River.

In 1753 most observers believed the source of the St. Marys River lay in the Okefenokee Swamp (Creek for "trembling earth" or "trembling water"), a great marshy wilderness in southeast Georgia. In 1772 De Brahm declared that the head of St. Marys River was *in* the Okefenokee. He, like his contemporaries, simply had no verification. Wright's map of 1763 indicated clearly that the St. Marys derived from the Great Swamp. In 1775 Dutch civil engineer Bernard A. Romans (ca.1720–ca.1784), employed by the government in British East Florida because of his service as deputy surveyor under De Brahm, represented the St. Marys River as having "a current of fine clear and wholesome water supplied from the pine lands through which it flows. . . . " He took this flow as substantiation that the river did not have its source in the Okefenokee Swamp. In 1776 Captain Romans indicated that the St. Marys River was the boundary separating British East Florida from Georgia.

After 1783, when British East Florida reverted to Spain, St. Marys River became an international boundary, and the determination of its head became a matter of great importance to the competing contiguous states. Bryan's knowledge of the area along with current maps, reinforced by mariners who also knew Georgia's tidal reaches, must have encompassed a good deal of accurate information mixed with hearsay. Andrew Ellicott's survey (1799) placed the source of St. Marys River outside the swamp, stating only that its dimensions "are yet but little known tho Certainly much less than have generally been Supposed." Not until the nineteenth century did surveyors decide that the head of only one branch of the St. Marys lay in the Okefenokee; the real head of the river is separated from the swamp by a high pine ridge. De Brahm, *History*, 18, 32; Romans, "Map"; Romans, *Natural History*, 1:36, 257; *Ellicott Journal*, map, "Southern Boundary of the United States," n.p.; Vignoles, *Observations*; Wright, *Georgia–Florida Frontier*, 1:Pt. 4, 16-17. See also Coulter, *Georgia Waters*, ch. 5; Hemperley, *Historic Indian Trails*, 80.

96. William Cooke or Cook (d. 1766) was an experienced military officer and engineer who served in the Royal Corps of Engineers. Under the Board of Ordnance this branch was separate from other army operations and had responsibility for "munitions, stores, and the technical services of artillery and engineers" (Marshall, 3). Cooke served as a lieutenant in 1707 and by 1722 held the rank of captain. On 25 August 1737 Oglethorpe commissioned Cooke the major of his regiment, and the Trustees approved a grant of 500 acres. That autumn Cooke presented the colony with a collection of sixteen

different cuttings of grape vines, which were forwarded to Frederica. The following year he commanded the Fort St. Simons's garrison at the island's south end. It was also during 1738, in April, that he acquired a house and lot in Savannah for his daughters Anne and Susan; a month later he petitioned the Trustees to permit his daughter Anne, when she came of age, to surrender her interest in the Savannah property ("lately belonging to Peter Gordon") to her sister Susan in exchange for "the house garden lot and farm lot in Frederica, which he would build & cultivate farther" (Egmont, *Journal*, 358; *CRG*, 29:271-72, 289).

In November 1739 Oglethorpe promoted Cooke to lieutenant-colonel. Apparently, though, the two men disagreed over tactics and possibly other matters, an argument leading to a strong personal animosity that boiled over in the summer of 1742. In June Cooke sailed for England, where he preferred charges against Oglethorpe the following year, and the War Office ordered the latter's return from Georgia for a court-martial. After he arrived in London in September 1743, his hearing (changed from a court-martial) was held 7–8 June 1744 before a Board of General Officers on charges of maltreatment and fraud. The board concluded by dismissing all charges against Oglethorpe, and within two weeks Cooke lost his commission for alleging "19 false groundless and malicious articles against his Colonel" (Ettinger, *Oglethorpe*, 252).

But this setback was not the end of Cooke's career. In 1746 he was appointed Chief Engineer in Newfoundland at twenty shillings a day, which, as Marshall points out, underscores the independence of Ordnance from the army. Cooke retired in 1751 and was succeeded by two engineers who "had five shillings deducted from their daily pay so that Cooke could be placed on half-pay." According to Connolly, Cooke died in London on 11 September 1766, but he may actually be the Colonel Cooke who, on 9 September 1766, was "returning in a Post-Chaise from Marshfield to Bath, [when] the Chaise was suddenly overturned by the Carelessness of the Driver, and the Colonel killed on the Spot." *Daily Advertiser* (London), 15 September 1766; *Gazetteer and Daily Advertiser* (London), and *London Evening-Post*, 16 September 1766; Marshall, "British Military Engineers", 3, 18; Clark, *Colonial Soldiers*, 974, 977, 981; Williams, "British-American Officers," 193; Egmont, *Journal*, 318, 345 (erroneously listed as C. Cook in the index); Egmont, *Diary*, 3:266, 300; *Gentleman's Magazine* 14 (1744): 336; *CRG*, 6:146, 29:241-42, 289; *Treasury Books and Papers*, 5:559; Connolly, *Royal Engineers*, 119; Ettinger, *Oglethorpe*, 250-53; Ivers, *British Drums*, 82, 134-37, 183-84; Ramsey, "Fort William," 511.

97. Galleys, among the earliest vessels in the Mediterranean, were shallow draft, oared warships with a single deck. Usually some 140 to 180 feet in length with main and foremasts, they had yards and sails similar to those of xebecs. Although galleys were unsuitable for rough seas, they were especially useful in calm coastal waters where most

fighting vessels could not maneuver in narrow passages and around sandbanks. Marquardt, *Rigs & Rigging*, 152-53; Falconer, *Dictionary*, 137.

98. Meaning *xabeque* (Spanish), *schebec* (German), or *xebec* (French), a small, fast, three-masted war vessel with sails and rudder, often used as corsairs in the Mediterranean, and especially good for tacking. Depending on the wind, the sails could be square-rigged on the foremast, lateen-rigged on the main and mizzen masts, or square-rigged on the main; if the craft was sailing close-hauled, a full lateen rig would be substituted. Grimm, *Deutsches Wörterbuch*; Marquardt, *Rigs & Rigging*, 149-50; *Steel's Elements of Mast-making*, 202-3; Falconer, *Dictionary*, 326.

99. Settee (saettia, scitie, cettea, etc.) was a single-decked Mediterranean vessel characterized by a long sharp prow, two or three masts, and lateen rigging. Marquardt, *Rigs & Rigging*, 145; Falconer, *Dictionary*, 260; *OED*.

100. On 15 September 1752 a great hurricane of unknown origin that hit Georgia and South Carolina, according to Ludlum, ranked "with Hugo (1989) and Andrew (1992) as the most severe that . . . ever struck the southeast Atlantic coast." In Charleston it had a devastating impact as the coincidence of high winds from an easterly direction and high tide produced a storm surge that sent water ten feet above the high-water mark, drowning people and livestock. Apparently, the storm's center passed just southwest of the city. In the aftermath "nothing was to be seen but ruins of houses [and] wrecks of boats." As the *South-Carolina Gazette* proclaimed, it was "the most violent and terrible HURRICANE that ever was felt in this province" (19 September 1752).

Savannah and environs suffered far less damage. The combination of a tide four feet lower than usual and wind coming from a land quarter evidently drove the water from both river and estuary toward the sea. Farther south along the Georgia coast some members of the Dorchester religious community went to survey a large grant of land, and the gale hit as their schooner lay in the harbor near St. Catherines Island. On 16 September, thwarted in their attempt to put to sea, they "went within land to Tibi [Tybee], where, meeting with high winds, they sailed up to Savannah." From there several of them returned home overland and found "in many places [the storm] left not one tree in twenty standing, and threw down many Buildings" (Stacy, *Midway*, 17).

A second hurricane two weeks later occurred on 1 October, impeding the remaining Dorchester group who "had a tedious, long passage" in their boat (Stacy, *Midway*, 17). Although residents of Charleston and Georgetown felt the effects of this gale, the greatest damage was in the Cape Fear region and Outer Banks of North Carolina. Dr. David M. Ludlum to Virginia S. Wood, 26 January 1993; Dr. Ronald C. Taylor, Division of Atmospheric Sciences, National Science Foundation, Washington DC, to Virginia S. Wood, 10 November 1992; Ludlum, *Hurricanes*, 44-48; Stacy, *Midway*, 17 (also quoted verbatim in Stevens, *History of Georgia*, 2:379); De Brahm, *Report*, 13, 99; Glen, *Colonial South Carolina*, 18-20; Milligan-Johnston, *Province of South-Carolina*, 18-20.

101. Bryan's reference to the ruins of a "large brick building" and the orange grove is puzzling, for apparently the Spanish did not resettle Amelia Island after Gov. James Moore's (?–1706) devastating raid of 1702. Yet while scouting there furtively in 1735, Oglethorpe saw peaches, oranges, myrtles, and vines flourishing. In the opinion of archaeologists, while it is possible that Highland Rangers occupied the old site of Fort San Carlos in 1741 when they were sent by Oglethorpe to establish a lookout, it is certain that they built no durable structure before being withdrawn in 1742.

During the early Spanish-aboriginal period, the coastal Georgia Indians became horticulturists only slowly and reluctantly; the first missionaries in the Guale area complained bitterly that the Indians neglected agriculture in favor of hunting and fishing. They occupied the islands sporadically (probably mostly during the winter), and their cyclical visits focused on gathering fish, shellfish, turtles, deer, and other wildlife. After contact with Spanish friars, Indians were occasionally observed cultivating small orchards near their villages.

Following the Indian uprisings, expulsion of the friars and destruction of their missions between 1665 and 1695, there remained vestiges of mestizo culture. Any Englishman who ventured into Spanish Florida was aware of it. In 1697 Jonathan Dickinson found the inhabitants of St. Augustine with large orchards that included "Plenty of Oranges, Lemons, Pome Citrons, Limes, Figs and Peaches." Many colonial Spaniards in Florida took Indian wives whose custom permitted them to reap rewards of fruit and crop cultivation. Spanish colonials living in St. Augustine experienced long delays in receiving supplies from Havana that caused actual hardship and under necessity traded with the Indians such as northern Timucuans who could speak Spanish. By the time the missions were abandoned, Timucuans, having learned there was a market for their produce, were cultivating the soil.

Although aboriginal food-gathering was not consistently gender-specific, archaeologists suggest that, in general, Indian women attended to agricultural activities. Since orange groves require much care, it may well be that women, Indian or mestiza, continued orange cultivation begun by the missions on Amelia Island. During 1950–1951 and 1963 archaeologists excavated the so-called "plaza lot" on the site of the seventeenth-century Spanish fortification Fort San Carlos, in Fernandina's Old Town near Amelia Island's northern tip. Spanish land records mention the "plaza" as the site of a famous "Naranjal," or orange grove, part of the plantation owned by Maria Mattair, who cultivated her large grove in 1784. It is possible that Bryan came across the ruins and orange groves of Fort San Carlos and mission Santa Maria, still visible in 1753; the "Naranjal" may indicate the Timucua-mestiza background of Maria Mattair. *Oglethorpe's Georgia*, 264; Smith, *Fort*

San Carlos, 14-15; Milanich, "Alachua Tradition," 47-55; Larson, *Aboriginal Subsistence*, 215; De Brahm, *Report*, 215; Larson, "Guale Indians"; *Dickinson's Journal*, 84-85, Appendix A, 154-62.

102. As early as 1670 British settlers in Carolina's Charles Towne made their first fortunes trading with the Indians—British goods for deerskins and Indian slaves. This trade spread rapidly, penetrating south Georgia and Florida by the 1680s. Since the Spanish did not arm their mission Indians, the traders proved to be a scourge against Indians in the provinces of Timucua, Apalachee, and Guale by constantly harassing them in slave-trading expeditions. By 1684 the Spanish mission in Guale (coastal Georgia) had collapsed.

Early during Queen Anne's War (1701–1713), the South Carolina Assembly authorized Gov. James Moore to capture St. Augustine before the French could send reinforcements to aid the Spanish. He failed to subdue the fort in 1702 but systematically pillaged all Spanish missions along the coast as far as St. Augustine; in 1704 he led what was probably the most devastating raid ever perpetrated against the southeastern Indians. Setting out on the Lower Trading Path through Georgia and Florida with fifty white and 1,000 Indian mercenaries, his force destroyed all but one of the fourteen missions; tortured and killed hundreds of Indians and Spanish; enslaved 325 men, women, and children; and relocated many more in South Carolina. Even after Moore's ruthless siege destroyed most of St. Augustine, the fort held. His actions resulted in opening the road to Louisiana, and Carolinians continued their raids in Florida for several years. By the 1720s there were only a few sparsely populated settlements clinging about the Castillo San Marcos in St. Augustine. *Expedition . . . Against the Spaniards*; Smith, *Fort San Carlos*, 14-15; Thomas, "Spanish Mission Experience," 72; Hudson, *Southeastern Indians*, 434-36; Deagan, "Spanish-American Colonization."

103. Oglethorpe evidently ordered construction of Amelia Fort at Saint Marys inlet in October 1736. It was a single wooden structure inside a stockade with five cannons. Ivers, *British Drums*, 78; *CRG*, 4:241.

104. Talbot, one of Florida's barrier islands, lies just south of Amelia Island and is separated from it by Nassau Sound; the mouth of the St. Johns River is directly south of Talbot. On De Brahm's 1770 map he indicated two distinct islands, Great and Little Talbot. De Brahm, *Report*, 200-201.

105. Fort St. George Island in Florida, formerly St. George Point, between the St. Johns River and Amelia Island, was separated from the latter by a creek. At the beginning of the eighteenth century, the Spanish called the entire coastal area of the Carolinas (and later, Georgia) "St. Georges." In May 1736, when Oglethorpe had a fort constructed at

the island's northeast side on a sixty-foot hill (now Mount Cornelia), British and Spanish considered it the southernmost point of the contested St. George's land. He located the fort on the site of an earlier fortification, where it functioned as a base camp from which patrol boats guarded the Inland Passage at its southern entrance. Following negotiations with the Spanish governor, Oglethorpe abandoned the fort in October. Three years later a small British detachment occupied it during Oglethorpe's abortive attempt to capture Fort Mose. For South Carolina as "San Jorge," see Pablo de Hita Salazar, Governor of Florida, to the Crown, March 6, 1680, with news of arrival of five Englishmen from the "province of Carolina, called St. George." Gallardo notes that previously the Spanish referred to the area as St. George: This was the first time they designated it Carolina. Gallardo, "Charles Town," 131-41 n. 3; *Dickinson's Journal*, 85; Crane, *Southern Frontier*, passim. For Fort St. George, see Ivers, *British Drums*, 62-64, 92, 105-6, 120; De Brahm, *Report*, 201, 204.

106. In 1748 Mark Carr and his son Thomas received adjacent grants of 500 acres each along the river Medway (now Midway). About a dozen other planters also took up grants along the river. Beginning in 1752 a group of Protestant Dissenters (Congregationalists) from Dorchester, South Carolina, arrived in the Midway District and settled on a site a few miles west of Carr's holdings where they established a church and community called Midway. (It was, in fact, halfway between the Savannah and Altamaha Rivers.) What both communities lacked was a focal point for trade—a marketplace and a port for shipping and receiving goods. It is clear from Bryan's journal that by 1753 Carr had planned a town on the site of his 500-acre tract. He sold lots to mercantile firms by 1757 or earlier, and by July that year the place he founded was called Sunbury. The following June he signed an indenture that established the town, and he named five commissioners. Sunbury became a designated port of entry with a customshouse; a church was also built, and the town was laid out in a grid with over 400 house lots. Sunbury is now among the dead towns of Georgia. Adjacent to it are the remains of Fort Morris and a museum, a historic site managed by the state. *CRG*, 18:91; Stacy, *Midway*, 14-35; Sheftall, *Sunbury*, 2-19; Jones, *Dead Towns*, 141-223.

107. Located in what is now Chatham County, Green Island is separated from Skidaway Island by Delegal Creek and on some modern maps appears to be a part of Skidaway. A crew of southern scouts from South Carolina built a base fort there about 1735. See Ivers, "Scouting the Inland Passage"; Ivers, *British Drums*, 53.

108. James Maxwell (ca. 1700–1768), planter and Indian trader, possibly from Pennsylvania, was in South Carolina by 1722. Between 1736 and 1751 he acquired by grant nearly 4,000 acres in Berkeley and Craven Counties, including a 1,600-acre headright along the Saluda River, part of a large tract deeded to the colony in 1747 by

headmen of the Lower Cherokee Towns. Elected to the Royal Assembly, off and on between 1737 and 1751, Maxwell also held other positions including tax collector and justice of the peace.

Maxwell was also South Carolina's appointed representative to the Cherokees, and among traders Meriwether considered him the "most important of them" during the 1740s. In mid-decade, when the price of rice dropped sharply during King George's War, Maxwell concentrated on raising cattle and within a few years owned a schooner for shipping rice. Although he was apparently wealthy, his assets were based on credit. When he was unable to pay a debt of £10,000 to his chief creditor, Charleston merchant Mathew Roche, the latter won a judgment against Maxwell, whose entire holdings (land, slaves, livestock, household goods, and schooner) were sold at auction on 22 January 1751. Roche purchased most of the property which he "turned over to Maxwell's wife Mary on a management basis" for ten years with an annual payment of interest. (Chesnutt, *South Carolina's Expansion*, 114; Dumont, *Colonial Georgia*, 30.)

There were further exigencies in April 1751 when news erupted that Indians murdered five white traders in South Carolina and threatened to kill all white people. For Maxwell's safety, friendly Indians urged him to leave. In Augusta he signed an affidavit concerning the crisis, and a copy was read before a meeting of the Georgia President and Assistants in Council. The following September, James Maxwell, "Brother to Mr. Audly [Audley] Maxwell of Midway River," attended a meeting of the Georgia Council "to view our Lands with an Intention . . . to settle in the Colony, if He could be accommodated. . . . [He has] about one Hundred Negroes . . . besides a large Family" (*GHQ* 36:69). Satisfied with his character and ability, the Council offered him any vacant lands of his choice. Maxwell purchased from John Milledge the 500-acre tract called Green Island and later purchased a 200-acre tract on the Midway River. Bryan's comment that Maxwell's house was too small no doubt reflected his straitened financial condition. Gradually, however, he recouped his fortune. He became justice of the peace in 1756 and in 1758 was among five trustees of the 300-acre tract conveyed by Mark Carr for the new town of Sunbury.

On 7 September 1722/1723 [sic], in St. Thomas and St. Dennis Parish, James Maxwell married Mary Simons (1701–1774), daughter of Benjamin and Mary Simons; the couple had several children. Maxwell died intestate in November 1768 at Midway "very much regretted by all who had the pleasure of his acquaintance" (*Ga Gaz*, 16 November 1768). In 1772 his widow made gifts of slaves to several of her children; her will dated 30 May 1770 in St. Philips Parish, Georgia, was probated 1 November 1774. Clute, *St. Thomas and St. Denis Parish*, 36; Chesnutt, *South Carolina's Expansion*, 113-15; Meriwether, *Expansion of SC*, 191-92; *CRG*, 6:697-98; 27:81, 88, 91; *BDSC*, 441-42; Clute, *St. Thomas and St. Denis Parish*, 36, 73, 82, 104; *Indian Affairs*, 19-20, 68-71, 83, 116-18, 172-73; Dumont, *Colonial Georgia*, 30; "Proceedings," 48-49, 69; Sheftall, *Sunbury*, 6-9, 186, 218; *Council Journal, 1753-1760*, 75, 87-88, 93, 161, 132; *Con-*

veyances C-1, see index; *Conveyances J*, see index; *Colonial Wills*, 92-93. According to family tradition the Maxwells were from the vicinity of Dumfries, Scotland (Cate Coll., Maxwell-McKay file, R419).

109. The Vernon River area was and still is considered a desirable location. In 1737 William Stephens (1672–1753), Secretary of the Georgia colony, was granted a tract there which he named Beaulieu (Bewlie). In early 1742 he wrote that "all the Trustees' Dutch [German] servants had long had their eyes on a piece of land between Hampstead and the Vernon River." The following September a group of them applied to the Board for grants at the place called White Bluff. Stephens, *Journal, 1741–1743*, 36; *CRG*, 4:664; 6:45-46.

110. For a comparison see the list of rivers and streams in De Brahm, *Report*, 145.

Credits

"Carte de la Nouvelle Georgie," from
Jacques Nicholas Bellin, *Le Petit Atlas Maritime*
(Paris, 1764), courtesy of Mary R. Bullard . . . . endsheets and jacket

Silhouette courtesy of Randolph Page Griffin
and Clayton Griffin, Atlanta, Georgia . . . . frontispiece

Courtesy of Cartographic Services, University of Georgia xiii

Courtesy of the Georgia Historical Society, Savannah xiv

Detail from the John De Brahm [*sic*] watercolor manuscript
"Map of Savannah River . . . ." (1752), courtesy of the Geography
and Map Division, Library of Congress (G3922.53 1752 .D4 Faden 45) 3

Courtesy of The von Reck Archive,
Royal Library of Denmark, Copenhagen (NKS 565.4) 6

Drawing by A. De Batz (1735), courtesy of the
Peabody Museum of Archaeology and Ethnology, Harvard University 9

From Mark Catesby, *The Natural History of Carolina,*
Florida and the Bahama Islands (1731–1743), vol. 2,
courtesy of the Rare Book Division, Library of Congress 10

Detail from John Gerar William De Brahm,
A Map of South Carolina and a part of Georgia . . .
(London: T. Jefferys, 1757), courtesy of the Geography
and Map Division, Library of Congress (G3910 1757 .DA Am .5-28) 13

From Andre Michaux, *Historie de Chenes de l'Amerique*
(Paris, 1801), courtesy of the Arnold Arboretum, Harvard University 21

From a manuscript in the Archivo General de Indias, Seville,
courtesy of the P.K. Yonge Library of Florida History, University of Florida 23

Detail from "The Profile of the Whole Citadelle
of Frederica . . . ," courtesy of the Hargrett Rare Book
and Manuscript Library, University of Georgia 26

Courtesy of The von Reck Archive,
Royal Library of Denmark, Copenhagen (NKS 565.4) 30-31

Fernandina Beach, Florida,
photographs by Sophie Ann Rice, courtesy of the photographer 53

Blackbeard Island, Georgia,
photograph by E. O. Mellinger, Bureau of Sport Fisheries and Wildlife 54

Blackbeard Island, Georgia,
photograph from the Bureau of Sport Fisheries and Wildlife 55

Cumberland Island, Georgia,
photograph by Nancy Coykendall, courtesy of the photographer 56

Index

Abbott family, 24

Abbott, William, n.78, n.80

Agricultural lands, potential for, 24, 27

Alachua Trail, importance of, 15

Altamaha River, 2, 4, 22, 34, n.73, n.76, n.89, n.106

Amelia Inlet, 28, 29,

Amelia Island, 28, 29, n.62, n.85, n.101, n.104, n.105

Amelia Fort, n.103

American Revolution, 14, 15, n.64

Apalachee, n.102

Apalachee Old Fields, 15, 27

Apalachicola River, n.2

Archaeological sites, n.67, n.71, n.73, n.84, n.101

Ashepoo River, n.1

Atlantic Islands, 8

Augusta, 2, 34, n.108

Bachelor's Redoubt, White Post, n.87

Bachelor's Redoubt (boat), n.87

Baillie, Kenneth, n.68

Baldwyn, Elizabeth, n.78

Ballimavee, village, n.91

Barnwell, Col. John, xv, n.18, n.73

Barriemackie, 28, n.91, n.93

Barrier islands, x, 2, 8, 11, 15; 53; n.85, n.94. *See also* specific names

Bath, England, n.96

Battle of Bloody Marsh, 24, n.86

Beaulieu (Bewlie) Plantation, n.109

Beaver Plantation, n.65

Bee, Thomas, n.63

Bellair, n.64

Benjehovah Bluff, n.70

Berkeley County, n.20, n.63, n.108

Bevan, Joseph Valence, xi

Beverages: citrus juices, 12, n.80; punch, 25, n.81, n.82; rum, n.18, n.81; wine, 12. *See also* Brewery

Bind Swamp [Bird Swamp?], n.63

Blackbeard Island, 54-55

Blyth Island, n.86

Board of Trade, n.6

Board of Ordnance, n.96

Boat crew, 5; character of, 5; 25; hardships endured, 32, n.95

Boats, armed scout boats, xii, 1, 4, 5, 7, 19, 25, n.61, n.105; canoes, 7, 20; galleys, 29, n.97; piragua (periaguas, periagua, periauger, pereauger), 1, 6, 7, n.33, n.34; schooners, n.100, n.108; settees, 29, n.99; and xabeques (schebec, xebec), 29, n.97, n.98

Boltzius, Johann Martin, pastor, n.64

Bosomworth, Abraham, n.68

Bosomworth, Adam, 5, 19-20, n.67, n.68

Bosomworth Controversy, xi-xii

Bosomworth family, 4

Bosomworth, Mary Musgrove, n.6, n.67

Bosomworth, Mr., 32

Bosomworth, Thomas, n.6, n.67, n.68

Bourbon Field, Sapelo Island, n.73

Bowler, William, n.91

Brampton plantation, n.2

Brewery (Brew-house), 27

Brick construction, 29, n.73, n.101

Brick Hill River, n.94

Brick Kiln River, n.95

British Army, n.79, n.84, n.86; Board of Ordnance, n.96

British East Florida, n.95

Broad River, 24

Brunswick, n.86, n.87, n.90

Bryan County, n.2, n.66

Bryan family, n.17

Bryan, James (brother), n.2

Bryan, James (son), n.17

Bryan, Janet (Cochran) (mother), n.2

Bryan, Jonathan, experienced outdoorsman, ix, xii, 1-2, 5; as an entrepreneur, ix; acquires and develops land, xi, xii, 1, 2; personal characteristics of, xii; motivation for the journey, 2, 7-8, 15; interest in developing Altamaha region, 15, 22; biographical note, n.2

Bryan, Joseph (father), n.2

Bryan, Joseph (brother), n.65

Bryan, Mary (Williamson) (wife), n.2
Bryar's Creek, n.64
Buffaloes, 9, 10, 27-28, 29, n.89
Buffalo Creek, n.89
Buffalo Ford, n.89
Buffalo River, n.89
Buffalo Swamp, n.89
Bulloch, James, n.61

Camden County, n.89
Cane swamps, 28
Cape Breton, Nova Scotia, n.6
Cape Fear region, n.100
Caribbean, 8, n.78
Carolinians, n.102
Carr, Jane (Perkins), n.86
Carr, Capt. Mark, commands armed scout boat, n.86; founder of Sunbury, 5, 32, n.86, n.106, n.108; 27; biographical note, n.86
Carr, Thomas, n.106
Carr's Fort, n.86
Carrs River, 27, 34
Carteret's Point, n.87
Castillo San Marcos, St. Augustine, n.102
Cattle. *See* livestock
Charleston (Charles Town), 12, n.64 n.65, n.73, n.102, n.100
Chatham County, n.107
Cherokees, n.79, n.108
Christ Church, Savannah, n.84
Christmas Creek, n.93
Clubb Creek, n.90
Coal mines, n.6
Coastal Georgia Historical Society and Museum of Coastal History, n.83
Colleton County, n.63, n.65
Combahee River, n.1
Cooke, Anne, n.96
Cooke, Susan, n.96
Cooke (Cook), Col. William, 29; invention of, n.92; biographical note, n.96
Corn, xv, 8, 11, 15, 19, 20, 22, n.44, n.67, n.84, n.86
Cotton, 12, n.61
Cowpens, 8

Craven County, n.108
Creeks, 15, 27, n.1, n.62, n.67, n.95
Creightons Island, n.71
Crieff, Scotland, n.61
Criollo cattle. *See* Livestock
Crooked River, n.94
Cumberland Island, ix-x, 5, 27, 28; description, 29; 56; n.64, n.79, n.85; fortified, n.91, n.92
Cumberland Sound, 32
Cuthbert, Capt. John, n.61

Darien, Isthmus of Panama, n.72
Darien, Scottish settlement, 4, 24, n.72, n.75; n.93
Davis, Caleb, n.80
Davis v. *Demere*, n.80
De Brahm, William, cartographer, military engineer, surveyor, ix, 2; biographical note, n.64; acquires land, ix, n.64; mistakes site of Fort St. Andrews, ix-x; illness, ix, 5, 7, 19, 28, 32, n.64; n.50, n.79, n.95; maps Georgia coast, n.64, n.70, n.71; maps Sapelo Island, n.83; maps Talbot Islands, n.104
Deer, 5, 11, 27-28, n.101. *See* Food, venison
Deerskin trade, 8, n.102
De Lancey family, merchants, n.6
Delaroche Creek, n.95
Delegal, Lt. Philip, n.83
Delegal Creek, n.107
Demere, Capt. Paul, n.79
Demere, Capt. Raymond, commands Fort Frederica, 25; n.64, biographical note; n.79; n.80
Demetre, Capt. Daniel, commands armed scout boat, 19, 25, 28; biographical note, n.62
Demetrius Bluff. *See* Harris Neck
Demetrius Island, description, n.71
Dickey, Capt. Alvin, Jr., n.94
Dickinson, Jonathan, n.101
Dissenters. *See* Religion
Dividings, n.90; description, n.94
Dividings Creek, n.95
Dividings River, ix-x, 28, 34, n.95
Doboy Inlet, 22
Doboy Island, 22

Doboy Sound, 22, n.71
Dominican friars, n.71
Doncaster, York, England, n.86
Dorchester, n.100, n.106
Dryden, John, n.39
DuBignon Creek, n.84
Dumfries, Scotland, n.108
Dunlop, Capt. William, n.67, n.73

East India Company, n.81
East Florida. *See* British East Florida; Spanish East Florida
Ebenezer, 4, n.64
Edisto River, n.1
Egg Island, 22
Egg Island Sound, 22
Egmont, Earl of, n.89
Ellicott, Andrew, n.95
Ellis, Gov. Henry, n.32
England, n.62, n.64, n.84
Entailment, 1
Environment, n.37

Farm equipment, 11
Fernandina's Old Town, n.101
Fish and fishing, 5, 8, 25, 27, 28, n.18, n.101; shellfish,
Fish Hawk Nest Ponds, n.86
Flaflagafga River. *See* St. Marys River, n.95
Flax, 12
Florida, 4, 12, 14, n.78, n.102
Floyd, Marmduke, xii
Floyd, M. H. and D. B., Collection, xii
Floyd, Picot, xii
Food: artichokes, n.73; barley, n.84; citrus fruit, n.73, n.101; figs, 12, n.73, n.101; garlic, n.73; nuts, 12; olives, 12; onions, n.73; peaches, n.73, n.101; peas, 11, 15; potatoes, 11; wheat, 11. *See also* Corn, Oranges, Rice, Fish, Game
Fort Augusta, 4
Fort Delegal, n. 83
Fort Frederica, 4; description, 24; 26; n.78, n.83, n.93
Fort King George, xv, n.73, n.76

Fort Loudoun, n.64, n.79
Fort Morris, n.106
Fort Mose, n.105
Fort Prince George, n.79
Fort Prince William. *See* Fort William
Fort San Carlos, n.101
Fort St. Andrews, site of, ix; condition of, 5; description, 28, 30-31, 32, n.64, n.91, n.93
Fort St. George, 32
Fort St. George Island, 5, n.105
Fort St. Simons, 25, n.83; n.92, n.96
Fort William, condition of, 5, 29; 28, 29; 32; n.91; description, n.92
France, territorial claim, 2; n.64, n.79
Franciscan mission, n.73
Franklin, Benjamin, n.44
Franks family, merchants, n.6
Frederica, ix, xi, 1, 5; 12, 15, 22, 24, 32; description, 4, 24; 24; 25; 26; 28, n.20, n.34, n.75, n.78, n.79; fire, n.79; "the Club," n.79; n.80, n.82, n.84, n.87 n.92, n.96
Frederica (scout boat), n.62
French Huguenots, n.79
Fresh Water Bluff, n.70
Freshet, 24, n.76
Fuentes, Francisco de, n.73

Game: 2, 5, n.67, n.101; bears, 28; raccoons, 32; venison, 5, 20, 28, 32; turtles, n.101. *See also* Buffaloes
George-Town ("the Elbow"). *See* Hardwick
Georgetown, n.100
Georgia, as alluded to by Bryan: 19, 24, 29, 32, 34; agricultural prospects, 11-12, 14-15; boundary with Florida, n.95; hurricane of 1752, 29, n.100; Indian trade, n.102;
Indian Lands, n.1; Inland Passage, n.90;
rivers of, 34.
Georgia, military units. *See* Military units, colonial
Georgia Historical Society, xii
Georgia Gazette, n.29
Georgia Trustees, 1, 4, 8, 12, n.64, n.78n, n.84, 89, n.96
Georgia-South Carolina boundary, 2

German Salzburgers, 4, 8, n.27, n. 64 n.75, n.109

Germany, n.64

Gibraltar, n.79

Glen, Gov. John, n.79

Glynn County, n.89

Goldsmith, Lt. Thomas, n.80

Gordon, Peter, n.96

Graham, Anne (Cuthbert), n.61

Graham, David, n.61

Graham, Patrick, n.61, n.66

Grammont, French pirate, n.73

Granville County, n.63

Grape vines, n.96

Graves, John, n.63

Graves, Sarah, n.63

Graves, William, n.63

Great Britain: Queen Anne's War, n.102; Anglo-Spanish War, 1; Commissioners of the Board of Trade and Plantations, 4, n.6, n.14, n.36; King George's War, 14, n.78, n.108; Privy Council, n.6, n.32; trade goods, 14, n.102; Parliament, 14

Great Cumberland Island, n.92

Great Ogeechee River, 19, 34

Great St. Simons Island, 22, 24

Great Satilla River, 24, 34, n.89

Great Talbot Island, n.104. *See also* Talbot Island.

Green Island, 5, 34; fortified, n.107

Guale, n.73, n.101, n.102

Guales, n.73

Habersham, James, n.61

Haddon, Richard, privateer, n.78

Half Moon Bluff, n.93

Hampstead, n.109

Hanover (scout boat), n.62

Harden, William, Col., n.1

Hardwick (Hardwicke), 19, n.62; recommended as capital, n.66, n.79

Hardwicke, First Earl of, n.66

Harrington Hall, n.79

Harrington, First Earl of, n.79

Harris, Ann (Cassell), n.62

Harris, Francis, n.61

Harris Neck, n.71

Harris, William, n.62

Hart, Richard, n.78

Havana, n.92, n.101

Hemp, 12

Herefordshire, England, n.84

Hermitage Island, n.86

Hermitage Plantation, n.86

Heron, Col. Alexander, n.86

Hext, Edward, n.65

Horton plantation, 5, 25, 27

Horton, Rebecca, n.84

Horton, Maj. William, commands Fort Frederica, 25, 27, n.82, n.84; biographical note, n.84; n.84; n.86

Hudson River, n.6

Hunting. *See* Game

Hurricanes, 5, 29, n.92, n.100

Hutchinson Island, 1

Iberia, 8

Illegal trade, n.78

Indentured servants, n.91

Indian Camp Bluff, n.70

Indian Lands, xi, 19, n.1

Indians, 2, 4, 7, 9, 20, 22, 27, n.71, n.73, n.79, n.101; treaties, 2, n.67, n.79; trade, 4, 8, n.102; warfare with, n.1, n.86, n.108; slaves, n.102. *See also* Creeks, Cherokees, Guales, Yamacraws, Yamassees, Timucuans

Indigo, xv, 8, 12, 14-15, 19-20, 22, n.59, n.84

Inland navigation. *See* Inland Passage

Inland Passage, 1, 7, 8, 28, n.90, n.92, n.93, n.94; n.105

Insects, 5, 11, 14

Intracoastal Waterway, n.90. *See also* Inland Passage

Inverness, Scotland, n.76

Italian Vaudois, 8

Jekyll Creek, 32, n.90

Jekyll Island, 4, 15, 25, 27, n.74, n.79, n.84

Jekyll, Sir Joseph, n.74

Jekyll Sound, 22, 27, 32, n.74

Jingle, Thomas, pirate, n.73

John Smith's Island. *See* Demetrius Island and Creightons Island, n.71

Jones, Noble, n.61

Joseph's Town, n.61

Journal, motivation for, xv

Journal, provenance, xi-xii; authorship, xii; description of, xv; editorial method, xv

Keowee treaty, n.79

Kimber, Edward, n.67, n.82, n.92

Laurens, Henry, merchant, 15

Laurens, Henry, n.84

Levy, Asher, n.6

Levy family, merchants, n.6

Levy, Isaac, merchant, xii; journal erroneously attributed to, xii, 34, n.6

Levy, Moses, n.6

Levy, Rachell, n.6

Levy, Sampson, n.6

Little Satilla River, 34

Little Sapelo Island, 22

Little Ogeechee River, 34

Little St. Simons Island, 22

Little Talbot Island, n.104

Livestock, xv, 2, 7, 8, 11, 15, 27, n.67, n.80, n.100, n.108; cattle, 8, 11, 15, 27, 29, n.67, n.84, n.86, n.108; hogs, 8, n.87; horses, 8, 27, 56, n.84, n.85

Logan, William, n.79, n.81, n.84, n.86

London, England, 4, 12, n.64, n.78, n.96; merchants, 14, n.6

London merchants, 14

Long Reach, n.65

Louisiana, n.102

Lower Cherokee Towns, n.108

Lower Trading Path, n.102

Lucea, Jamaica, n.78

Ludlum, David M., n.100

McIntosh, Col. William, n.89

McIntosh County, n.72

McIntosh family, Scottish settlers, 20, n.72

Mackay, Hugh, Jr., n.91

Mackays Town, n.91, n.93

Mackintosh. *See* McIntosh

Marine Company of Boatmen, n.86

Marshes of Mackay, n.87

Marshfield, England, n.96

Marshlands, 8, 11, 12, 19, 22

Maryland, n.86

Mattair, Maria, n.101

Maxwell, Audley, n.108

Maxwell family, 5, 34

Maxwell, James, planter and Indian trader, visit to, 34, n.68; biographical note, n.108

Maxwell, Mary, n.68

Maxwell, Mary (Simons), n.108

Medicinal plants, 12

Mexico, n.73

Midway, 34, n.68, n.86, n.106

Midway Church, n.63

Midway River, 34, n.108

Military units, colonial: Georgia, 5, 24, 27, 80, n.79, n.84, n.86, n.87, n.88, n.93, n.96, n.101; South Carolina, n.1, n.79

Milledge, John, n.108

Miller, Robert, botanist, 14

Mission Santa Catalina (plan), 23

Moore, Francis, n.20, n.34

Moore, Gov. James, 29, n.101, n.102

Mount Cornelia, n.105

Mud River, 22

Mulberry Grove Plantation, n.61

Mulberry trees, n.61

Myerhoffer, Henry, n.78

Myrtle, n.101

"Naranjal," n.101

Nassau Sound, n.104

Naval stores, 15

New York, merchants, xii; n.2, n.6, n.78

Newfoundland, n.96

Newport District, n.62

Newport River, 4, 20, 34, n.63. *See also* North Newport River; Serpent River

Nicholson, Gov. Francis, xv

North Newport River, n.68, n.70, n.71

Ockmulgee River, 24

Oconee River, 24

Ogeechee River, 12

Oglethorpe, James Edward, 1, 2, 5, 24, 28, 29, 32, n.67, n.68, n.74, n.75, n.76, n.78, n.81, n.84, n.85, n.89, n.91, n.101; constructs fortifications, n.83, n.93, n.103, n.105; regiment, n.79, n.84, n.86, n.79, n.91, n.93, n.96

Okefenokee Swamp, n.95

Oranges, 8, 12, 14, 25, 27, 29, n.73, n.82, n.79, n.101. *See also* Food (citrus fruit)

Ordinance, 4, 25, n.36, n.83, n.62, n.92, n.96, n.103; Cooke's invention, n.92

Oré, Father Luis Geronimo de, n.73

Ossabaw Inlet, 19

Ossabaw Island, xii, 34

Ossabaw Sound, n.90

Outer Banks, n.100

Pallachucola Creek, n.1

Paris, France, n.86

Pemberton, James, n.79, n.84, n.86

Pennsylvania, n.108

Penny (Penney), Sgt. James, 25, n.80

Perkins, Roger, n.86

Piraguas. *See* Boats

Philadelphia, n.6, n.64, n.79

Pilotage, 15, 27, n.92

Pinckney, Eliza (Lucas), 14

Pipemakers Bluff, n.1

piragua (periagua, periauger, pereauger), n.33

Pirates, n.73

Plantation Creek, n.90

Planters, character of, 12

Plug Point Plantation, n.86

Pocotaligo settlement, n.1

Poetry, 4, 8, 19, n.39

Pope, Alexander, n.39

Port Royal, 1, n.2, n.72, n.73

Postell, Andrew, n.65

Powell, Capt. James Edward, n.80

Pratt, Thomas, n.62

Prince George (scout boat), n.62

Prince William Augustus, Duke of Cumberland, n.92

Prince William Parish, n.1, n.63, n.65

Prince William Sound, n.92

Prince William's Fort. *See* Fort William, n.92

Pringle, Robert, exports orange products, 12

Privateering, n.78

Province of Guale, n.73

Purrysburgh settlement, n.1

Pye, John, n.84

Quebec, Canada, n.6

Ramsay, William, n.92

Redford, Perthshire, Scotland, n.61

Religion, xii, 8, n.106; Moravians, 8; Presbyterians, n.1, n.2, n.84; Congregationalists, n.63, n.100, n.106; Lutherans (Salzburgers), 4, n.64. *See also* Spanish Missions

Reyes, Juan Ygnacio de los, n.91

Reynolds, Gov. John, xi, 2, n. 36, n.66

Rice, x, xv, 1, 5, 8, 11-12, 14, 19, 20, 22, 29, n.61, n.108

River Swamps, 22

Robinson, Pickering, n.61

Roche, Mathew, n.108

Romans, Bernard A., n.95

Romerly Marsh, n.90

Royal Navy, 14

Royal Corps of Engineers, n.96

St. Andrews Parish, n.63

St. Andrews Sound, 27

St. Augustine, 1, 2, n.62, n.73, n.78, n.86, n,92, n.101, n.102

St. Catherines Island, xii, 4, 5, 8; description, 19, 32, 34, n.67, n.100

St. Catherines Sound, 19

St. Dennis Parish, n.68, n.108

St. George Island, 32

St. George Point, n.105

St. Georges, n.105

St. Helena Parish, n.1, n.20, n.65, n.84

St. John Parish, n.63, n.68

St. Johns River, 1, 2, 5, 15, 25; description, 28-29; 32, 34, n.62, n.104, n.105
St. Marys Inlet, n.103
St. Marys River, 15, 34, n.90, n.95
St. Philips Parish, n.108
St. Simons Island, xi, 1, 4, 15, n. 62; n.75, n.79, n.86; description of, n.83. *See also* Frederica, Fort Frederica, Fort St. Simons
St. Simons Point, 25
St. Thomas Parish, n.68, n.108
St. Tillet River. *See* Satilla River
Salter, Thomas, n.62
Salter, Anna Cassell, n.62
Saluda River, n.108
San Miguel de Guadalpe, n.71
San José de Zápela, n.73
Santa Maria, n.101
Sapelo Indians, n.73
Sapelo Island, xii, 4, 20; description of, 22, 34, n.62, n.71, n.73.
Sapelo River, 20, 27, 34, n.71
Sapelo Sound, n.71
Satilla River, 27
Savannah, 1, 4, 12, 19, n.34, n,61, n.67, n.84, n.96, n.100, n.106
Savannah River, 1, 2, 4, 12, 34, n.2, n.61, n.64, n.65
Schooner Landing, n.88
Scottish settlers, 24, n.61, n.68, n.72, n.76
Scouts, xii, 5, n.18, n.62, 1.101, n.107
Serpent River, ix, n.70, n.71
Settees. *See* Boats
Sheftall, Levi, n.6, n.84
Silk, 12, n.61
Simmons, Elizabeth, n.63
Simmons, John, Jr., n.63
Simmons, John, n.63
Simmons, Sarah, n.63
Simmons, Thomas, n.63
Simmons, William, planter, ix, x, 2, 19; intended settlement of, 4, 20, 63, n.71
Simmons, William, 28
Simons, Mary, n.108
Simons, Benjamin, n.108
Skidaway Island, n.90, n.107

Skidaway Narrows, n.90
Skimmer, 33
Slafea-Gufea River, 28, n.94, n.95
Slaves, ix, 11, 12, 20, n.24, n.50, n.63, n.67, n.68, n.71, n.80, n.108
Society of Free Masons, Savannah, n.62
South Carolina, x, ix, xi, 4, 8, 11, 14, 15, 19, n.67, n.79, n.83, n.84, n.86, n.101, n.102, n.107
South Newport, n.63
South Newport River, 34, n.70
South-Carolina Gazette, n.39, n.64, n.100
Southampton, n.68
Spalding, Thomas, n.79, n.89
Spanish 2, 7, 8, 22, 24, 25, 27, n. 62, n.71, n.83, n.92; missions, 23, n.67, n.71, n.73, n.101, n.102
Spanish East Florida, 1, 4, 15, n.95, n.101
Stanhope, Col. William. *See* Harrington, First Earl of
Stephens, William, n.61, n.109
Stevens, William Bacon, xi-xii
Stewart, Ens. Alexander, n.92
Stoney Creek, n.1, n.63
Sunbury, 32; n.63, n.86, n.106
Swamp lands, 11, 12, 22, 27, 28, 29
Swiss Grisons, 8
Symmonds (ship), n.84

Tabby construction, 4, 24, 27, n.26, n.84
Talbot Island, 5, 32, n.104
Tea Kettle Creek, 22
Tefft, Israel Keech, xi-xii
Telfair Academy, n.2
Tennessee River, n.79
Thlathlothlagupka River. *See* St. Marys River, n.95
Timber, resources, 4, 7, 15, 27; for boat and ship building, 7, 15, 20, n.61, n.69; cedar, 7, 27, 28, 29; cypress, 7, 15, 20; live oak, 19, 21; 25, 27, n.69; pine, 2, 4, 15; oak, 29; tupelo, 20; white oak, 28, 29 (staves)
Timucua, n.102
Timucuans, n.101
Tobacco, n.86

Tomochichi Mico, 1, n.89
Turtle River, n.86, n.89
Tybee Island, n.90, n.100

U.S. Army Corps of Engineers, n.90
Urlsperger, Samuel, Bishop of Augsberg, n.64

Vernon River, 34, n.109
Vice-Admiralty Court, Frederica, n.86
Virginia, n.86
von Münch, Christian, n.64
von Brahm, William. *See* De Brahm, William

Walnut Hill Plantation, xi, 1, 19
Wassaw, n.90
Weather conditions, xii, 5, 15, 19, 20, 28, 29,
    32, n.32, n.73. *See also* Hurricanes
Wesley, Charles, n.84
Wesley, John, n.84
West Indies, n.32

White Bluff, n.109
White Post, 27, n.87
Whitefield, George, n.2
William, John, Jr., n.65
Williamson, John (brother-in-law), 2, 19, 28;
    biographical note, n.65
Williamson, Magdelene (Postell), n.65
Williamson, Mary (Bower), n.65
Williamson, Benjamin, n.65
Wolf Island, 22
Wright, Gov. James, 15

Yamacraws, n.67, n.89
Yamassees, 1, n.1, n.73, n.86
Yonge, Henry, n.64, n.66
Yorke, Philip. *See* Hardwicke, First Earl of
Young, Eliza Ruth, n.68
Young, Elizabeth (Maxwell) Bosomworth, n.68

Xabeques (Schebec, Xebec). *See* Boats

Notes on the Contributors

VIRGINIA STEELE WOOD, a native of North Carolina, is the reference specialist in naval and maritime history at the Library of Congress, Washington, D.C. She received her under-graduate degree from the University of North Carolina at Greensboro, a master's degree from Boston University, and a master's degree in library science from Catholic University of America in Washington. For several generations her family lived along the Georgia coast (her mother was born on St. Simons Island). In addition to her award-winning book, *Live Oaking: Southern Timber for Tall Ships*, Virginia Wood has edited for publication early dairies and other historical documents that concern coastal Georgia.

MARY RICKETSON BULLARD was born in Boston to archaeologist parents who lived in Massachusetts and Guatemala. She was graduated from Barnard College (B.A., 1948) and Harvard University's School of Education (M.A.T., 1950). She later worked at the University of Pennsylvania's archaeological sites of Tikal and Quirigua in Guatemala. With her archaeologist husband, William Rotch Bullard (Harvard, Ph.D., 1960), she lived for several years in Belize. Widowed at an early age, she turned her attention to the Sea Islands of Georgia. She has written several articles and books about Cumberland Island, the home of her father and grandparents.

R. Edisto

R. Ascepoo

Edmonsbury

Radnor

Riv. Salchatchers

Riv. de Port Royal

Beaufort

Fort Frederic

R. Aldborough

R. May

Parisbury

Entrée de St Helene

I St Helene

Cap St Michel

Port Royal

I Trench

I Dayfuskie

I Tibee

I Wilmington

I Wassa

I Ossabaw

I. de St Catherine

Ebenesel

Vieux Ebenasa

Abercorn

Joseph Town

Savannah

F. Argyll

R. du Roi George

Darien

Fort Moore

N. Augusta

Chicasaw

Chicasaw

Riv. Savannah

Crique Bryard

Riv. Ogechee

Riv. Oconce

Riv. Alatahama

ou R. George

la Fourche

R. Ocone

R. Ucmulgee

N O U V E L L E

G E O R G I E

Latitude   Septentrionale

20

10   D.

33

60

40

30

20

10

32

60